THE FATE OF THE LAKES
A Portrait of the Great Lakes

Text and Photographs by James P. Barry

BAKER BOOK HOUSE Grand Rapids, Michigan

For my Mother
who has long known the Lakes

Low is the lake, and brown the withered reeds;
No sails lean northward gleaming with new spray;
No children's laughter thrills the long chill day;
White oaks, unshawled, are shaken bare of seeds.
Far on the stony beach the migrants reign,
Harsh-tongued wild duck, their glittering feathers preen
And ripple the cold blue lake with their cold green—
And flashing brittle light, wing south again.
Wild duck, wild duck, unknown what lands you range
While my dumb trees wait patiently for frost,
But I know orders, crowns and loves are lost
In such brief news of life's one victor—change:
Seasons I cross, as you, and have recrossed,
Yet your mailed wings are this year final, strange.

Robert Bhain Campbell, "Orders, Crowns and Loves"

Used by permission from Holt, Rinehart and Winston, Inc.

CONTENTS

Lake freighter in the lower Saint Lawrence on a foggy day. Three-fourths of the trade through the Seaway is between ports on the Saint Lawrence River or the Gulf of Saint Lawrence and ports on the Great Lakes. Much of it is carried in vessels such as this.

1. down to the sea

From Lake Ontario to the natural head of seaborne navigation at Montreal, the Saint Lawrence Seaway comprises seven locks, forming a watery staircase to lift and lower the ships. Five of the seven are Canadian; only two-sevenths of the Seaway belongs to the United States. If to the five Canadian locks along the Saint Lawrence one adds the eight locks of the Welland Canal that carry ships between Lakes Erie and Ontario, thirteen-fifteenths of the system is Canadian. This fact sometimes becomes obscured during American debates over Seaway policies.

The history of the Seaway underlines its basically Canadian nature. Not until the Canadian government in the 1950s began to move openly toward building the Seaway by itself did the United States become a reluctant partner. When President Eisenhower decided to back American participation he not only had to placate such obvious opponents of the project as the East Coast ports and the railroad interests, but even had to convert such a spokesman for the Great Lakes states as Sen. Everett Dirksen of Illinois. (John Kennedy became the first Massachusetts senator in many years to back the Seaway idea, explaining that New England finally had to recognize the legitimate needs of other areas.)

Before the Seaway was built, the Saint Lawrence canal system that carried small vessels between the Lakes and Montreal was entirely Canadian, and the little ships that used it were almost entirely Canadian. Commerce of the Great Lakes throughout much of their history has been pulled in two directions: toward Montreal or toward New York and the eastern United States. Montreal was

Two lakers pass in the Seaway, the one downbound (on the right) carrying grain and the one upbound carrying ore. A great economic advantage of the Seaway is that vessels can carry cargoes through it in both directions and thus avoid expensive return trips empty.

first on the scene, and during the era of canoes and bateaux it clearly dominated Great Lakes commerce. But as sailing vessels and steamers developed, it began to fall behind, mainly because Canada did not initially build the canals needed to carry ships through the waterway. She was not so much loath to spend the money as she was afraid of attack by her expanding neighbor to the south. Why put canals where invading armies could seize or destroy them? But in 1825, when the Erie Canal was completed, Great Lakes commerce drained away through it to New York as though a stopper had suddenly been pulled from a great tub. Canada belatedly started building the various canals that became the early ancestors of the modern Seaway.

Through the years many other factors have complicated the issue, but the most basic conflict still is geographical: shall freight be carried to and from the Great Lakes region by (now) rail and truck connections with the East Coast or by water connections with Montreal and the seas beyond? (Ironically, Montreal itself did not see it this way in the 1920s and 30s; its businessmen feared that the Seaway would ruin its position as a major port, and they took much the same stance as the New Yorkers.) Geography also gives Americans and Canadians rather different visions of the Seaway. Americans usually look upon it as a way to bring ocean shipping into the Lakes. Canadians, many of whose most populous regions lie along the waterway, are more apt to see it as a route for domestic commerce. In fact, that is its primary function today; only about one-quarter of the tonnage that passes through the Seaway is bound for or coming from overseas ports.

One of the great advantages of the Seaway is that it allows bulk cargoes to be carried both ways, called "backhauls."

In a typical Seaway voyage a lake freighter picks up iron ore on the Gulf of Saint Lawrence and carries it to a lake port such as Conneaut, Ohio; she then proceeds to Chicago, Duluth, or Thunder Bay empty, loads grain and returns down the Lakes and the Seaway, discharging the grain at a Gulf of Saint Lawrence port. There or nearby she picks up ore again and repeats the cycle. In this way she is unproductive for only a small part of the trip. This pattern may also allow

Typical Seaway lock, looking upstream. The gates are just opening to let a vessel move out of the lock.

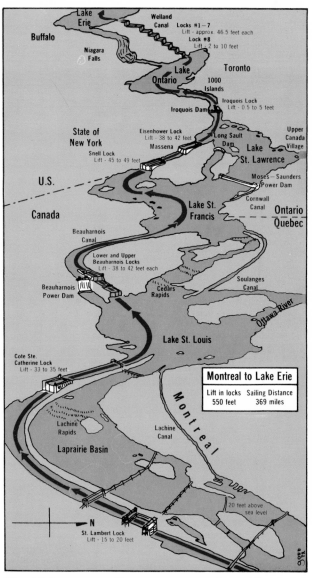

The St. Lawrence Seaway as seen from Montreal

After the map by A. G. Ballert

Labels on map:

Lake Erie
Buffalo
Welland Canal Locks #1–7 Lift - approx. 46.5 feet each
Lock #8 Lift - 2 to 10 feet
Niagara Falls
Lake Ontario
Toronto
1000 Islands
Iroquois Lock Lift - 0.5 to 5 feet
Iroquois Dam
State of New York
Eisenhower Lock Lift - 38 to 42 feet
Long Sault Dam
Massena
Lake St. Lawrence
Upper Canada Village
Snell Lock Lift - 45 to 49 feet
U.S.
Canada
Moses – Saunders Power Dam
Cornwall Canal
Ontario
Quebec
Lake St. Francis
Beauharnois Canal
Lower and Upper Beauharnois Locks Lift - 38 to 42 feet each
Beauharnois Power Dam
Cedars Rapids
Soulanges Canal
Ottawa River
Lake St. Louis
Cote Ste. Catherine Lock Lift - 33 to 35 feet
Montreal
Lachine Rapids
Lachine Canal
Laprairie Basin
20 feet above sea level
N
St. Lambert Lock Lift - 15 to 20 feet

Montreal to Lake Erie

Lift in locks	Sailing Distance
550 feet	369 miles

subsidiary rail service to have its back-hauls. At Conneaut, for example, the trains that carry the ore inland to Pittsburgh bring back coal for use in the Great Lakes area. By contrast, lake freighters that carry ore from the Lake Superior region to steel mills on Lake Michigan or Lake Erie usually return empty.

In the course of a year the vessels using the Seaway pass back and forth many times, and the crews learn to recognize the minor peculiarities of each lock, even though to the casual traveler all locks look much alike. One story tells of a chief engineer who had drunk so much liquor that he collapsed, bottle in hand, into his bunk as his ship was passing through one of the locks. On the return voyage, a week later, he finally came to. He heard the typical noises of a ship locking through: the electrically amplified commands of the lockmaster and the grinding of winches. He opened one eye groggily, tried to shake the fog from his head, then rose and stumbled to a porthole. It was the same lock. "What!" he said. "Haven't we moved out of here *yet?*"

The quarter of Seaway traffic that represents overseas tonnage threatens to shrink drastically. Roughly half of it is general cargo. (Broadly speaking, general cargo consists of manufactured or processed goods in relatively small lots, as opposed to bulk cargoes such as ore, coal, or grain, which usually move by the shipload. General cargo is the most profitable cargo.) On the ocean there has been a revolution in the handling of this cargo, and the impact upon lake ports could be serious. Since 1966, many ocean vessels carrying such cargo either have been rebuilt to handle containers or have been designed specifically as container ships. These containers are metal boxes in standard sizes that can be moved readily by truck or rail and transferred quickly from one mode of transport to another. The ease with which they can be transferred and the protection of their contents from pilferage and damage have considerably reduced cargo handling costs — or so their proponents say.

Claims have been made that containers save as much as 90 percent of cargo-handling costs. There is a strong opposing view, however. The head of one cargo terminal snorted, "They're just a fad — I give them five years." Among their disadvantages is the fact that often they must sit unused on the dockside until they are needed; during this time they earn no return for their investment. Sometimes they must even be shipped back empty to their owners, at considerable expense in labor and ship space. Another port administrator raised the question, "Who pays for the containers?" He pointed out that despite the supposed

cargo-handling savings, the cost of goods had not been reduced; obviously the cost of building and maintaining the containers was being passed on. Furthermore, not all cargo can be handled in these containers. Some of it is too large, or it may be damaged by the tendency of the containers to become damp inside from condensed moisture. The administrator's conclusion was that the only people who really benefit from using containers are the shipowners: their vessels can be loaded and unloaded more quickly with them and thus can make more voyages in a given time and earn more money.

But whatever the good and bad features of containers, at present they dominate general ocean cargo. To take full advantage of the container system, most of the ships built for the trade are large,

Ocean general-cargo freighter at Toledo. The Seaway is also a means for ocean ships to reach Great Lakes ports. This is the smaller part of its function, but the one that receives most attention.

and all of the ships handling such cargo spend as little time as possible in port. The big ships, however, cannot pass through the Seaway, and even the smaller ships will lose money if they must call at several ports. Some of the lines that have operated conventional cargo vessels into the Lakes have ended their services because they can no longer compete with rail and truck shipment of containers to the East Coast for rapid transfer to container ships. Others continue, however, many of them carrying conventional freight in their holds and containers on their decks.

Lake ports are adapting to the handling of containers. At Toronto harbor (above) is a special container crane built to order in Germany, a container, and the bow of a ship. Ships that were not originally designed for containers still can carry them as deck cargo, as does this one (below) in Milwaukee harbor.

And there have been encouraging signs that the problems posed to lake ports by containers can be solved. New semicontainer ships have appeared, such as the *Transamerica* and the *Transcanada* of the German Poseidon Lines; these vessels are equipped to handle containers, conventional freight, some bulk freight, and refrigerated cargo. Therefore they may be able to operate profitably with the mixture of overseas cargoes that normally move through lake ports. The British shipping firm Manchester Liners recently began to operate small container ships between Montreal and the lake ports. These vessels pick up containers and carry them to Montreal for shipment overseas aboard large container ships; on their return trips the smaller vessels bring back containers with cargoes for the Lakes. This service moves containers between Manchester and Detroit in eleven days and between Manchester and Chicago in thirteen. At the same time, the Head-Donaldson Line began to operate two container ships, each with a capacity of about 160 containers, directly between Toronto and ports in the United Kingdom.

Another answer is a development of the container idea known as the "lighter-aboard-ship" concept, or LASH. Several experimental LASH ships are now building on the ocean. Instead of trans-

HAPAG-LLOYD

porting containers as we now know them, these vessels will carry lighters, which in effect will be floating containers. The lighters will be floated to the ship in one harbor and stowed aboard, then unloaded in another harbor and floated away again. Such lighters could be moved by tug to and from one or two major lake ports where LASH ships called. One can visualize groups of lighters being moved through the Seaway in the manner of barge tows on the Mississippi, and then loaded aboard large ocean-going LASH ships at Montreal.

Lake ports are willing to expend great effort to attract and retain ocean shipping. This was not always so. When the Seaway first opened in 1959, people of the Great Lakes region were not at all certain that they wanted ocean ships on their waterways. The "salties," as fresh-water sailors call ocean seamen and ocean freighters, were not used to ship-handling in narrow channels; and as a result they bashed into everything from lock walls to other ships. Sedate inhabitants of lake ports were shocked to find that some of their teen-age girls were staying all night aboard the foreign vessels. And the captain of one ship, entering a major harbor where there were no preparations to handle ocean shipping, asked with sarcasm if perhaps the people hadn't expected ships?

Small container vessels now trade through the Seaway, transferring containers to and from ocean-going container ships at Montreal. This vessel is in Milwaukee harbor.

Today ocean ships still find it tricky to move about on the Lakes, and not infrequently they get stuck sideways in narrow channels. But they are quickly forgiven. Newspaper stories now explain that only "adult women" go aboard visiting ships — and then of course only with the captain's permission. And the major ports are racing to install container-handling equipment and to do whatever else may be possible to lure overseas cargoes.

Most of the proposed methods of handling general cargo, however, do not solve the problem of time. Speed often is crucial. When rapid delivery is necessary, no shipper will choose a mode of transport with the delays caused by movement of containers or lighters from one lake port to another and thence through the Seaway for further transfer at Montreal. If direct container service through the Seaway is available, he may use that. Otherwise he will choose rail or truck carriage directly to the Atlantic coast. It is doubtful if even the semicontainer ships can compete in this high-priority market, for they need time to load their other types of cargo and they may be forced to call at several ports to deliver and pick up full loads. Thus although methods are being found to move general cargo through the Seaway in manners that are compatible with present-day ocean shipping, there surely will continue to be an overland flow of high priority merchandise to and from the Great Lakes area. At present, although 25 percent of United States high value overseas cargo originates in the Great Lakes region, only 5 percent is shipped through lake ports. Probably the best that those ports can hope for is a modest increase.

About half of the foreign tonnage that now passes through the Seaway is made up of bulk cargoes. Large amounts of scrap iron and steel pass down the Saint Lawrence to foreign ports. Grain also moves out of the Lakes in some quantity, bound in foreign freighters to overseas destinations. These overseas bulk trades fluctuate according to world demands for the materials carried and according to world demands for shipping, but it seems likely that they will continue their somewhat erratic patterns into the future.

The Seaway faces another serious problem: it is usable only about eight months of the year. From early December to mid-April it is closed by ice. For one-third of the year shippers must find alternate means of moving their goods. No doubt some of them find it most convenient to use the same mode of transport year around and do not even consider shipment by water.

Much thought is now being given to ways by which the navigational season can be lengthened both on the Seaway and on the Lakes. Historically, the Great Lakes developed a type of ship called the icebreaker that was designed to smash through ice, permitting navigation earlier and later than the normal season. Among the first of such vessels was the Canadian steamer *Chief Justice Robinson,* which operated on Lake Ontario in the 1840s and carried both freight and passengers. One traveler described the ladies and

Container arriving by truck at the Port of Toledo. Also note general cargo in boxes and crates being loaded in background.

Lake freighter leaving a Seaway lock upward bound.

gentlemen aboard enjoying the luxuries of "a regular drawing-room," in which there were flowers and paintings. On Lake Michigan since before the turn of the century, railroad car ferries built as icebreakers have operated throughout the winter. Today both the United States and Canadian governments maintain icebreakers on the Lakes. The largest of these vessels, the U.S.C.G.C. *Mackinaw* — the "Mighty Mac" to Lake sailors — was the most powerful in the world when she was launched at Toledo in 1944. Since then, however, the

Scandinavian countries have moved far ahead of us, and Americans now study Scandinavian methods of keeping ships moving in winter. The U.S. Maritime Commission has even retained the Wartsila Shipbuilding Company of Helsinki, Finland, to conduct tests toward extended-season navigation on the Lakes.

The U.S. Coast Guard and the U.S. Corps of Engineers have concluded that it is technically feasible to extend the Great Lakes–Saint Lawrence navigation even to a full twelve months. It would require more and larger icebreakers than we now have. It would also require methods of keeping locks and lock gates free of ice. And above all it would require money. Money to aid navigation on the Great Lakes and Saint Lawrence has always been in short supply, but recently a number of industries in the lake region have gathered together to work for improvements and to see that the Lakes and the Seaway receive a fair proportion of government aid. They have formed what is known as the Industrial Users Group. Among them are companies with both national prestige and economic muscle. Some of the first members were the Ford Motor Company, the Dow Chemical Company, the Chrysler Corporation, Great Lakes Steel, Imperial Oil, and Canadian Industries. The Industrial Users Group is pushing for a greatly expanded navigational sea-

Ships from three oceans, Milwaukee harbor. From left to right, an Indian, German, and Greek ship.

son, and it seems probable that they will get it. Recently James M. Scovic, Chairman of the Group (and manager of Purchasing and Distribution for the Midland Division of Dow Chemical), announced that talk forecasting that the Seaway would be kept open all winter by the year 2000 was a "copout." Said Scovic, "The Seaway should be open the full twelve months within the next few years."

Mention Seaway tolls to an American lake skipper and you get a sulfurous rejoinder that no tolls are charged on other waterways maintained by the U.S. government, whether they are the approaches to coastal harbors, the Mississippi River, or even the canal at Sault Sainte Marie. But one Canadian shipmaster probably spoke for the majority of his fellows. "Why," he asked, "should we pay so that the shipping companies can make bigger profits?" To him "we" simply meant the taxpayers. The principle of charging tolls was agreed upon when the United States and Canada first decided to go ahead with construction of the Seaway. In the United States, which had had a policy of free government waterways, the tolls were a sop to the Seaway's enemies. In Canada, the smaller country that was building most of the system, tolls seemed economically necessary.

The perpetual problem of the Seaway has been its finances. In theory, the Seaway charges tolls that are used to pay its operating expenses, pay interest on its debt, and contribute toward retirement of that debt. In fact, the tolls do not bring in enough revenue to make all of those theoretical payments. In 1969, ten years after it was opened, the U.S. section of the Seaway took in about $5.8 million in tolls, but even so, it suffered a net loss of about $7.5 million during the year. The Canadian part of the Seaway between Ontario and Montreal took in about $15.6 million in tolls and had a net loss of about $8.6 million; the Welland Canal, which to Canadians is an integral part of the Seaway, took in about $2.5 million in tolls and had a net loss of $7.9 million.

Finances might not have become such a problem but for the rocketing inflation that followed the waterway's opening. In its first ten years, operating expenses increased 162 percent. (Economic developments during this time also drove the great Penn–Central Railroad into bankruptcy and led the airlines to cut services and lay off employees.) In December of 1969, the *Wall Street Journal,* a financial publication based at New York on the Eastern Seaboard, announced in a front-page article that the Seaway "looks like a flop at this point." The article, which ignored the primary

Iron ore is mined in Labrador and northern Quebec and shipped by rail to ports on the Gulf of Saint Lawrence where it is loaded aboard lake freighters to carry to Great Lakes region steel mills. In this early evening photo a conveyor-belt loading machine pours ore into the open hatch of a laker. The man who controls the loading sits in the cab where the light shows on the upper part of the machine.

bulk-freight trade, concentrated upon the shrinking general-cargo trade and the growing debt, and quoted a Seaway "backer" as predicting that the waterway "may just go to pot." Although an uncharitable reader might think that the *Journal's* tears had a certain flavor of crocodile, by late 1969 it was becoming evident that the Seaway did face problems. It was time for the two governments who owned the waterway to provide it some measure of financial relief.

The awakening regional consciousness of the Great Lakes area that led to formation of the Industrial Users Group was also reflected in the Great Lakes Conference of Senators, a body which helped to pass the Nixon maritime program, firmly establishing the U.S. shores of the Great Lakes as a seacoast region. These senators also looked with cold eyes at the financial burden of the Seaway, including the 6¼ percent interest charged on its debt.

When the American Merchant Marine Bill was passed in 1970, it contained an amendment that wiped out all present and future interest payments by the American agency, the Saint Lawrence

The Seaway moves through history. The oldest buildings of this mission on the Caughnawaga Indian Reserve date from 1725. Many of the men from this reserve are high-steel workers who construct bridges and skyscrapers.

A sounding barge, pushed by a tug. Government barges of this type constantly check the depths of water in the Seaway channels.

Seaway Development Corporation. At the same time, Secretary of Transportation John A. Volpe announced that the bill would insure that there was no increase in Seaway tolls. Loud hosannas arose along the American shores of the Great Lakes.

On the Canadian side, however, there was polite silence. The Saint Lawrence Seaway Authority, the Canadian administrative body, had commissioned an analysis of the Seaway by a firm of consulting economists, D. Wm. Carr and Associates. The Authority did this because it was looking forward to discussions with the United States on the subject of tolls, and it wanted the study as economic background. The Carr Report was sent to the president of the Seaway Authority at the end of October 1970; it was published in book form early in 1971. Pending its release, the Canadians said nothing.

The report, however, significantly stated: "Broadly, the United States opposition to 'any increase in the present tolls on the Seaway,' seems to overlook the fact that Canada already carries a comparatively excessive share of the deficits related to financing and operating the Seaway and that failure to increase tolls means that Canada would be forced to carry an increasingly larger share of such deficits." Mr. Carr went on to add, "The unilateral United States decision on

Interior of the Canada Steamship Lines package freight terminal at Hamilton, Ontario, showing typical general cargo in barrels, boxes, and bales. This terminal, on Lake Ontario, ships and receives domestic general freight moving between ports on both the Seaway and the Lakes.

A lake freighter waits to enter a Seaway lock. Crews of ships waiting here have decorated the top of this wall and many others along the Seaway.

matters ordinarily reserved for joint negotiation marks a significant departure"; and he suggested that Canada withdraw from joint negotiations and set up her own tolls.

The Carr Report also recommended that Canada provide financial relief for the Seaway, but that it be done in rather a different manner than the United States had followed. The repayment of the basic cost of the Seaway, the report contended, did not make good economic sense. The government had paid for the waterway, the government would continue to own the waterway, and there seemed to be little point in going through the motions of retiring the debt. Furthermore, private entrepreneurs remained in good standing if they merely paid interest on their debts without returning any part of the principal; why should a public enterprise operate differently? Therefore the report suggested that Canada make no further attempt to recover the initial investment as long as the Seaway maintained itself and continued to pay its interest, and the report recommended that tolls be raised "moderately" in an effort to arrive at this point.

Thus the United States and Canada have taken almost exactly opposite stands on financing the Seaway. Both governments, however, have an obvious interest in keeping the waterway in operation. Perhaps Canada has a greater interest than the United States, for there are people in the United States who would not be unhappy to see the Seaway become an abandoned ruin, marked only here and there by plaques calling attention to spots of historical interest; and a further turn of the political kaleidoscope could bring these people to the fore again. But it is difficult to imagine that Canada would raise tolls to the extent that would cause a serious decline in Seaway use.

Over the years the Saint Lawrence canal system that preceded the Seaway was rebuilt several times to permit larger vessels to pass through it. In its final form it could accommodate the little ships known as "canallers" — typical lake freighters in miniature, with a maximum length of 259 feet and a cargo capacity of about 2,600 short tons. It also could accommodate small general-cargo ocean freighters with a capacity of about 1,600 short tons. We may contrast such vessels with the ships that the Seaway now handles: lake freighters of 730 feet in length, 75 feet in beam, and a capacity of 28,000 short tons; ocean bulk carriers of over 700 feet in length and a capacity of 23,000 short tons; and ocean general-cargo ships averaging 460 feet in length with capacities of about 8,000 short tons.

But today it is more to the point to contrast vessels passing through the Seaway with vessels now operating on the Great Lakes and the ocean. On the Lakes, a new generation of 1,000-foot freighters is emerging; on the ocean, container ships are being built that are 944 feet overall and 105.5 feet in breadth (container ships must be wide to provide stability for their high deck loads). As a result, pressure is growing for rebuilding the Seaway to accommodate such vessels. In historical perspective, this would simply be one more in the series of rebuildings of the various Saint Lawrence canals that have allowed the passage of larger and more efficient ships.

It would also no doubt be by far the most expensive rebuilding to date, and it is not difficult to foresee that all of the anti-Seaway forces in the United States would be most displeased to have large amounts of money spent on the enlargement of a transportation system that does not pay its debts — or at least, on such a system that is not under their control. Perhaps more to the point is the question of Canadian reaction to the idea, for Canada owns practically all of the waterway; and we have seen before that when Canada makes a firm decision on construction, the United States, however reluctantly, is apt to follow. Perhaps the best indication of Canadian

On the wall above the Beauharnois Locks, a deckhand stands holding a light line attached to a heavier cable that will go over the bright-colored bollard.

A vessel of the maximum size to use the Seaway — 730 feet long and 75 feet wide — enters a lock, showing the close fit.

thinking is the Carr Report, which forecasts that the capacity of the Seaway facilities will not be a limitation until about 1985, and which suggests various ways to make the present Seaway more efficient: greater use of current maximum size vessels, reduction of transit times, lengthening of the season, and "some easing of institutional limitations," a phrase that seems to mean better handling of strikes and walkouts. It also suggests that planning and construction for post-1985 requirements should begin about 1975.

Therefore in the long run a further increase in the size of the Seaway locks and channels seems likely. The United States led the way in 1970 by opening the enlarged Poe Lock at Sault Sainte Marie, with a capacity for vessels 1,000 feet long, 105 feet in beam, and 29 feet in draft. Although the Sault canal, the most active in the world, is internal to the Great Lakes and thus largely exempt from the slings and arrows of the anti-Seaway forces, in a larger sense it is part of the Seaway system. If the Poe Lock is successful it will certainly influence developments along the Seaway proper.

Throughout the coming years, the Seaway will remain more a way for lake vessels to go down to the sea than for ocean vessels to come up to the Lakes;

In the upper Saint Lawrence, an upbound lake freighter with a cargo of ore, as seen from a downbound freighter with a cargo of grain. Domestic bulk freight traffic will continue to be the major trade on the Seaway in the foreseeable future.

Loaded with ore, the freighters head toward the Seaway. Here a laker moves up the Saint Lawrence.

domestic trade will be the major trade, just as it now is. The waterway also will be mainly a bulk-freight route. Some domestic general cargo — "package freight" in lakes parlance — will continue to use the Seaway and may even increase if the winter freeze-up is shortened. The profit and glamor of overseas general cargo will make lake ports and planners try hard to capture more of it, but they will have a rough fight against geography and economics. Even if they are moderately successful, the Seaway tonnages will remain overwhelmingly of grain, ore, scrap metal, and similar bulk commodities.

Seaway finances will no doubt continue troubled. The two governments will be forced to absorb much of the initial cost of the project. About the best that anyone can hope for is that the Seaway will earn a little more than its bare operating expenses. In an era that has seen the financial collapse or near-collapse of other major transportation systems, the problem is neither unique nor surprising. It does, however, make the waterway vulnerable to the political winds of any given moment; and that in turn makes difficult any judgment of the government help or harassment that the Seaway may receive in the long term.

Nonetheless its operations will continue to become more efficient. In 1970, it handled fifty million tons for the first time, and since then tonnages have exceeded that figure. The most obvious and immediate moves will be to keep the system open for a larger part of the year. We may also see improved mechanical and electronic means for passing ships through more quickly. And in time there almost certainly will be an enlargement of Seaway locks and channels so that they can take bigger vessels than they do now.

Japanese freighter bound up the Saint Lawrence above the Beauharnois Locks.

Snell Lock, one of the two U.S. locks of the Seaway, as it appears at 1:00 a.m. from a ship about to enter it.

A self-unloading bulk freighter. This is a bulk freight vessel with the additional equipment that permits her to unload herself. The boom carrying an endless belt rides on deck when the vessel is under way, then in port swings out for unloading. Self-unloaders are increasingly popular.

2. the lakers

From the Gulf of Saint Lawrence to the head of Lake Superior we find them — the slab-sided, box-shaped, beautiful vessels called "lakers." They carry the bulk cargoes of the Great Lakes–Saint Lawrence River system along the two-thousand-mile marine highway that runs from the Atlantic into northeastern and central North America. The lake freighter is a specialized ship developed to meet conditions found on these waters. It is quite different from the usual ocean-going cargo ship; when one occasionally sees in a distant salt-water port a lake freighter that somehow has strayed into ocean trade, there still is no question as to where and how she began her career. The flat sides; wheelhouse in the bows; long, open deck; engine room in the stern — all these are the marks recognized the world over, of the Great Lakes freighter.

The freighters are beautifully designed for the particular work they do. The long, flat sides fit closely into canal locks and carry the maximum cargoes through them; the straight, unbroken decks give the dockside loading and unloading equipment free access to the bulk-cargo holds; the wheelhouse in the bows puts the wheelsman and the officer on watch in a position where they have the best possible view in narrow waters and in foggy going. The men who handle them know their qualities. Recently the attention of a freighter captain was called to another passing ship, one of a number on the Lakes that have their wheelhouses at the after end of the vessel, looking forward over the long deck. Why was she built that way? He rubbed his thumb and fingers together in the gesture that means money: "Cheaper to build." What did he think of her?

He shook his head. "I wouldn't want to sail her." The classic design for lake freighters will probably be with us for a long time to come.

The modern thousand-foot-long ships of the Lakes have the same recognizable features as the first lake freighter ever launched, the *R. J. Hackett,* which slid into the water at Cleveland, Ohio, in 1869. She was made of wood by the master builder Eli Peck, and she was only 211 feet long; but in her, Peck had devised the lake freighter as we know it today. She had the wheelhouse in the bows, the engine aft, and the flat-sided hull. Before her he had built a number of the schooners that were the first bulk carriers of the Lakes. These sailing vessels also had boxy hulls that enabled them to carry maximum cargoes through narrow channels and canals. Like sailing vessels the world over, they had living quarters in their forecastles and aft under their quarterdecks. What the ingenious Peck did was to put a steamship bow and stern on such a hull, install the wheelhouse forward and the engine aft in the two areas where the crew had always lived, and thereby he invented the lake freighter. The *Hackett* and the others that soon followed even had three or four masts and set sails when the wind was fair. Over the past century, the wooden hulls changed to iron and the iron to steel; the sails disappeared, and the masts dwindled in size and moved to the ends of the ships, where today they carry only lights, radio antennas, and flags. The sailing vessel bowsprit became the characteristic steering pole, the light spar that juts outward and upward from the bow of most lakers, so that the helmsman in his forward wheelhouse has an object ahead of him that he can line up on navigational markers.

As with any design, there are a few compromises and disadvantages. Lake freighters carry their lifeboats near the stern, atop their after cabin structures. (Because of this they usually carry inflatable life rafts forward as well.) Most of the deck crew — who man those boats in an emergency — are berthed forward under the wheelhouse. When it is necessary to launch the boats, the crew must hurry aft to do so. During a summer passage on one freighter the young wife of the first mate was enjoying her initial voyage. Her husband neglected to tell her that there was to be a boat drill, which his duties required him to supervise. Suddenly bells began to ring and the whistle began to blow; anxiously she looked for her husband, only to see him sprinting dramatically away from her along the deck, putting on a life preserver as he and his men ran for the boats — apparently completely abandoning her to a watery fate.

Boat drills are not merely tiresome formalities; like any vessels that travel navigable waters, lakers are subject to peril. Usually it strikes in the open Lakes. The most famous example is the storm of November 9 in 1913, which destroyed nineteen vessels, including two small ocean freighters and a lightship, and damaged twenty others, with a total loss of life of 251 people. The greatest losses at that time occurred in the open waters of Lake Huron, though every lake except Ontario saw a part of the catastrophe.

But disaster lurks in each curve of a channel, as the men who sail through them well know. The 350-foot Canadian freighter *Eastcliffe Hall,* bound up the Saint Lawrence on July 13, 1970, with a cargo of pig iron from Sorel, Quebec, for Saginaw, Michigan, tore out her bottom on the base of an old lighthouse. The ship was about six miles west of Massena, New York, at about 3:00 in the morning, when she missed a turn in the channel and ran onto a mud bank. She worked herself free from the mud, radioed that she was in no danger, and started back to the channel. As Patrick Tollins, one of the survivors, told the Associated Press:

About fifteen minutes later we really hit hard. The people below decks didn't stand a chance. We went down bow first in a matter of minutes.

Control station in the engine room of a lake freighter.

The forepeak filled with water and the men on deck started running toward the lifeboats. We tried to clear the boats but couldn't because of the angle of the deck.

She started to slide forward again as though she had slipped off a shelf, and the men started jumping off the stern.

She sank in about three minutes. Two men caught in the engine room were shot up through the skylights by the suddenly compressed air, and were saved. Nine people were lost, among them the captain and his nineteen-year-old son who was accompanying him on this voyage, and the chief engineer with his wife and six-year-old daughter.

By current standards the *Eastcliffe Hall* was a small vessel. Nearly all of the present Great Lakes fleet of some 250 bulk carriers are larger. She was built in 1954 as a "canaller," one of the little freighters designed to pass through the old Saint Lawrence canals before the Seaway was constructed. In 1959, she was lengthened by ninety feet, and her sides were raised three feet nine inches, so that she would be able to carry more cargo through the Seaway locks. Several other of the newer canallers received the same treatment to keep them in service.

These are comparatively new ships. Three-fourths of the present lake fleet are older. Steel vessels last much longer on the Lakes than do those on salt water; but even so, the age of many lakers is

A mail boat meets every vessel that passes Detroit and sends up mail by placing it in a bucket attached to a line.

*Large modern
freighter in the Saint Clair River.*

*In the wheelhouse of a freighter moving
up Lake Superior during a heavy
fog. From left to right are the first mate,
the captain, the fourth mate
standing at a radar screen, and the
wheelsman watching the gyro control.*

Typical lake freighter with wheelhouse forward and engine aft, with the long open deck between, and with flat sides to gain the most space in locks. Such vessels carry the bulk freight that makes up most Great Lakes cargoes.

astounding. Over eighty of the Great Lakes vessels of all types now in use were built before 1910. One launched in 1891 is still in service at this writing. Because of the considerable age of lake freighters, more and more of them go out of service each year. In 1970, The Marine Historical Society of Detroit, a group of people who religiously follow shipping developments, published a listing of new vessels of all kinds that had been placed in operation on the Great Lakes over the preceding fifteen years and of old vessels removed from operation during that time. The new ships took up sixteen pages, the old ones, seventy.

The Canadian government in recent years has subsidized the building of ships. After the Saint Lawrence Seaway was opened in 1959, a new group of freighters was built to the maximum dimensions permitted by Seaway locks: 730 feet long and 75 feet in beam. Before that, the largest freighters on the Lakes had been just over 600 feet in length. Because of the Canadian subsidies, almost all of the vessels built to Seaway size were Canadian. Today over thirty of the maximum size Seaway freighters are Canadian; only six are American. It is not surprising when a deck officer on a handsome new Canadian maximum size Seaway freighter looks over the rail at an old American freighter nearby, remarks upon the junk the Americans are sailing, and wonders how long the U.S. fleet will last. Most of the owners of this junk have been wondering the same thing.

Part of the answer to their problem lies in what surely was the oddest vessel the Great Lakes have seen, a motor ship officially called *Hull 1173* and unofficially known as "Stubby." Stubby arrived in the Great Lakes in June 1970, after a voyage up the Atlantic Coast from the Pascagoula, Mississippi shipyard of Litton Industries. She consisted of the bow and stern sections of a giant new freighter, welded together without any of the cargo hull that normally would stretch between, and also minus some of the tanks that would normally increase the beam of the vessel. Down one side of this tall, narrow, box-like object was painted a dotted line with the words "cut here" — as one observer noted, "just like a giant cereal package."

Stubby proceeded to Erie, Pennsylvania, to another Litton shipyard, Erie Marine, where a new idea in U.S. shipbuilding, a kind of mass production hull factory, was putting together the 815-foot middle part of the new vessel. Stubby was cut apart on the dotted line, just as the instructions said; and the two parts were welded in place to become the bow and stern of the largest lake freighter yet, 1,000 feet long and 105 feet in beam. In completed form she is much too big to go through the Seaway or the Welland Canal between Lakes Erie and Ontario, but since the recent enlargement of the Sault Sainte Marie Canal she is able to travel the upper four of the five Great Lakes. The *Stewart J. Cort,* as the completed ship was named, went into service in 1972 carrying ore for her owners, the Bethlehem Steel Corporation. On her first working voyage, early that May, she broke all Great Lakes cargo records by carrying 49,343 gross tons of iron ore from Taconite Harbor, Minnesota, to Burns Harbor, Indiana. She is the first of the next generation of freighters, the thousand-footers of the 70s.

Despite new methods of construction, shipbuilding in these days costs tremendous amounts of money; and until recently, shipowners on the U.S. side of the Lakes were hard put to find that money. In October 1970, Congress enacted legislation that should put American construction on a par with that on the Canadian side. It permits shipping lines to establish tax deferred construction reserve funds, something allowed U.S. ocean ship operators for a number of years. It raised the ceiling on government insured ship mortgages to three billion dollars. And in more general terms it recognizes the Great Lakes as a fourth seacoast, allowing ship operators

Typical lake freighter, Lake Huron.

Deckhands at work, Lake Huron.

The first thousand-foot-long freighter on the Lakes, the Stewart J. Cort,
has the typical flat sides and the typical laker arrangement of houses forward
and aft of the long open deck. Here she lies at Erie, Pennsylvania, where she was
built. This vessel is a self-unloader of unique design. She has a short
unloading boom on each side; when not in use the booms retract into the after
structure. When they are needed they move out of the rectangular houses on
either side aft. One such house is at the far right corner of the hull in
this picture. The control house for unloading is just forward of the twin stacks.

there any government benefits available to ocean shipping. This legislation should insure a healthy U.S. fleet.

Around the Lakes, the rapid loading and unloading of bulk cargoes has been developed into an art. A primary reason for the long, unbroken decks of lake freighters is to give dockside loading and unloading equipment a free sweep. The best-known unloaders are the Huletts, named for George Hulett, an eccentric Cleveland, Ohio genius who designed them and built the first one in 1898. George Hulett has been described as looking like a bullfrog in a baggy suit. He chewed tobacco and he spat juice during the conferences with tycoons of his day. But Hulett designed several important pieces of industrial equipment — the most striking is his unloader.

Engineers said Hulett's unloader couldn't work, but it did. It consists of large bucket jaws attached beneath a control cab, which is on the end of a long, steel arm connected by other arms to a massive base that rides on multiple rails on the dock. The jaws, together with the man who operates them, ride down into the hold, take a big bite of the cargo, and ride up again. They then move over the dock and release the cargo — usually iron ore — into a chute in the base. The chute funnels it either into waiting rail cars or into a large pit behind the dock.

To this day most ore-unloading ports on the Lakes are equipped with Hulett unloaders, which are still by far the fastest and most efficient pieces of unloading machinery. In today's market, however, it would cost several millions to build a new Hulett; and the old ones, though they seem indestructible and still give excellent service, are gradually becoming too small. The vessels of present maximum Seaway size are so wide that Hulett unloaders have difficulty in reaching across their 75-foot width and getting into the far corners of their cargo holds. The problems that would arise with a thousand-footer having a 105-foot beam are obvious. Clamshell unloaders of various kinds have been developed, which drop by cable from overhead structures. They are less expensive to build than Huletts, and most new installations have acquired them instead. But unless they are handled with utmost skill they are apt to damage the ship they are unloading, and they shower its deck with the lubricants necessary to keep them working.

Today the processed ores such as taconite are of uniform consistency; they are the increasing cargoes; and they can be handled readily by self-unloading equipment on the ships, a job previously not as feasible. As a result, the *Cort* and another big new U.S. ship, the 858-foot *Roger Blough,* are fitted with improved

self-unloading machinery. Self-unloaders, which in the past have operated mainly in specialized trades, have usually been considered a type apart from the regular bulk freighters that are unloaded by dockside equipment; but in fact they are specialized bulk freighters equipped with additional machinery. Now it seems probable that self-unloaders will gradually become the standard bulk carriers for transporting ore.

Loading processes are also changing, particularly in the ore trade. The high, dramatic ore docks are becoming things of the past, although a number are still in use. Hopper rail cars are run out on these high docks, and careful mixtures of natural ore are dumped into the pockets below, from which in turn the ore is run by gravity into the holds of ore carriers. Men who work on such docks, especially during cold weather when the footing is treacherous, have to be a nimble lot; one slip and they can find themselves down below in an ore pocket, quite possibly with more ore coming in on top of them.

But most of the big docks aren't high enough for even the 730-footers, let alone the thousand-footers. Their tops still rise well above the deck level of these ships, but the chutes at the bottoms of the pockets do not. In addition, the

At Thunder Bay, Ontario, government inspectors constantly take samples of the grain being loaded into the holds of freighters.

Lake freighter loading coal at Toledo for the steel mills of Detroit.
The coal-loading machine picks up entire rail cars and turns them over to
dump their contents in the chute.

high-grade ores that need to be mixed carefully have largely given way to lower-grade ores that are put through an initial processing near the mines, which results in uniform quality and needs no mixing. Such ores, which usually come in the form of marble sized pellets, are on occasion still run through the older kind of dock; but more often these days they are loaded by automated conveyer belt systems operated by a man who sits quietly at a control panel, looking down from a glassed-in vantage point. The conveyer belts can be set at levels that enable them to load the biggest ships. Some of the newest big vessels have cargo hatches that are much smaller than has recently been necessary; they are loaded by conveyer belts and they unload themselves, so there is no need for a big hatch to let in globs of ore from a pocket dock or to admit dockside unloading equipment.

Coal loading is now handled in much the same way as ore. Only the loading of grain remains about as it has for many years, probably because grain-loading techniques were for a long time more advanced than those for heavier cargoes. Grain is moved about in tall elevators by conveyer systems, then shot down chutes from the elevator bins to the ship's cargo holds. It is unloaded by hollow legs that are let down from the receiving elevators into the holds. These legs contain rapidly moving endless chains of small buckets that carry the grain upward into the elevator.

As grain is loaded into the ships, inspectors sample it with small scoops on the ends of long handles to make certain that the quality is constant. In the largest grain-handling port on the Lakes — and probably the largest in the world — Thunder Bay, Ontario (a city at the northwestern corner of Lake Superior that was formed in 1970 by combining the older Canadian cities of Fort William and Port Arthur), inspectors from both the Canadian government and the grain elevators work on each ship while she is loading and sample the grain that flows into the holds. One of the government inspectors wryly remarked that his job was to prevent the grain from falling below the specified standard whereas the job of his counterpart working for the elevator was to prevent it from rising above the specified standard.

Inevitably the elevators find themselves with some low-quality grain in their bins. Frequently their way of moving it on is to dribble it in tiny amounts into the main stream of good grain flowing into the holds. A government inspector, going to work at an elevator where he had not been before, asked one of the elevator workers about the whistle signals that were used there.

Hulett unloaders, the best-known pieces of unloading equipment, seen here at Conneaut, Ohio. The Hulett in the middle, with its jaws wide open, is going down into the hold under control of the man in the cab above the jaws. The far Hulett is down in the hold. The near one with jaws closed is carrying a bite of ore up from the hold to dump it ashore.

In the hold. An open-jawed Hulett is about to take a bite of ore while a bulldozer, which has been let down into the hold pushes more ore toward the Hulett.

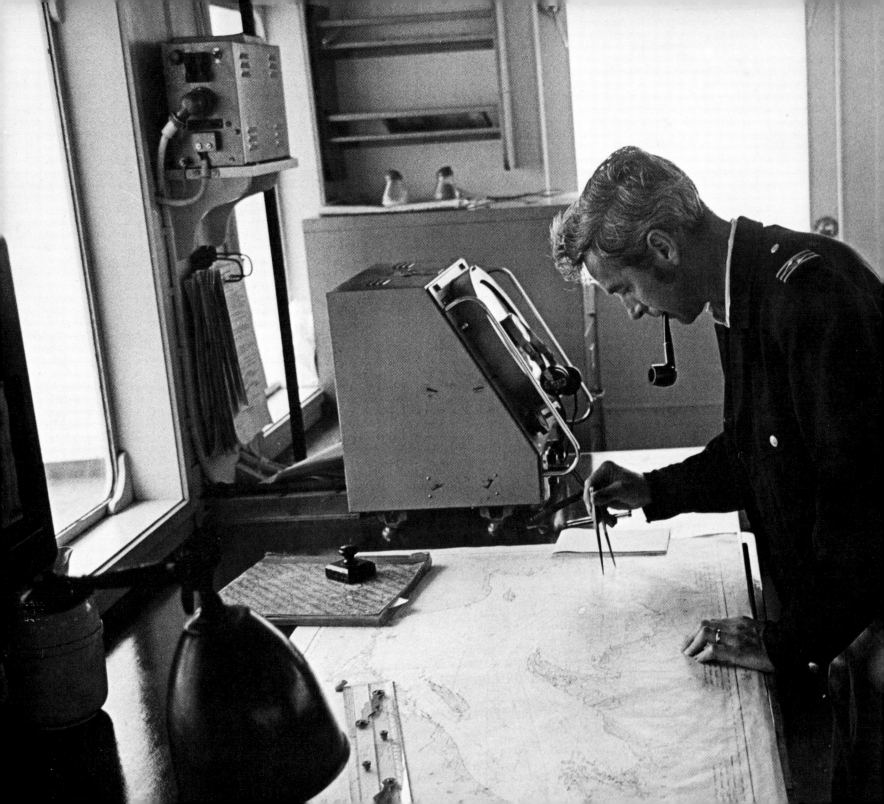

"One toot of the whistle means to start the flow of grain, two means to speed it up, and three means to stop it," the worker told him.

The government man, deciding that his new acquaintance was not too smart, asked with a straight face, "What does four blasts of the whistle mean?"

"Oh, that's the signal to speed up the dribble," said the other man.

"And five blasts?"

"To slow down the dribble."

But ships do not spend most of their time loading and unloading, at least not if they earn their way. The advanced cargo-handling techniques that are used on the Lakes are designed to speed the hours in port and let the vessels spend more time at sea. And that is how one likes to think of them: snoring along in the open lake, rising a little to the long swells, with the clouds and seagulls overhead for company.

There are days like that, when the crew works on deck in the sunshine. There are also, however, gray days when the ship is pounding into a heavy sea and the sky overhead is bleak. And there are stormy days. In November of 1966, shortly after Thanksgiving Day, the freighter *Daniel J. Morrell,* upbound in Lake Huron, was caught in an autumn storm, snapped in two and sank before even a radiotelephone message

could be sent. Of the thirty-three people aboard her, only one was saved. The *Morrell* was a sturdy 600-footer, a typical laker, which had been built in 1906. Perhaps her steel had become old and fatigued; a sister ship, caught in the same blow, had her deck plates cracked and was retired from service. But age is not necessarily the answer. The comparatively new 678-foot freighter *John O. McKellar,* driving into Lake Superior seas one night and taking solid water over her bows, cracked across the deck about 3:00 A.M. with a sound like a gunshot. The cracks occurred between one of the hatches and each side of the ship. Throughout the rest of that harrowing night and the next day, as the crew maneuvered her carefully into port — expecting that at any moment she would go the way the *Morrell* had gone — no further damage occurred. She was repaired and still is in service.

The construction of a steel lake freighter is flexible, unlike that of most ocean freighters. The reason for this is that the proportion of hull depth to beam is different in the two kinds of ships. Perhaps the best analogy is a steel ruler: place it on edge, so that it is deep like an ocean ship, and you cannot bend it up and down; but place it flat, so that it is shallow in proportion to its length as is a laker, and it can be flexed. If you stand at one end of a lake vessel while

The first officer of a freighter determines his ship's position at the chart table in the wheelhouse.

As the boom swings out, the man is lowered toward the dock.

When his feet touch the dock the deckhand steps away from the seat.

Lakers constantly approach docks or canal walls where there is no person on shore to handle their lines. They have developed a quick way of putting deckhands ashore. Just aft of the forward structure on each side a boom is mounted. Attached to the boom is a line with wooden seat. The deckhand, wearing a lifejacket, sits on the wooden seat and is swung out over the side.

she is moving through long swells, you can observe the flexing of the hull. From the bow looking aft, for example, it is evident that the stern rises and falls in relation to the midships deck and that the relatively shallow hull of the vessel acts as a giant spring. The give that occurs amounts to only a few feet and can be seen only when one stands in the right position, but it is a striking phenomenon.

Most saltwater seamen are not familiar with this characteristic of lake vessels. One Newfoundlander who had signed on a laker was completely unaware of it. One night when the ship was traveling through a heavy sea he was unable to sleep because of a steady, loud squeaking. He rose and went out on deck, where he found that the noise was caused by one of the rails that supported the deck crane; the rail was rubbing against its mount. Most of the newer lakers carry small electric deck cranes to lift and move their large, heavy steel hatch covers. These cranes are fastened down when the ship is under way; but in port they move forward and aft along the deck, straddling the hatches and moving on two railroad rails, one on each side. The rails, which run the length of the deck, are mounted in such a way that when the hull flexes the rails are permitted to move slightly; otherwise they would snap. The deckhand did not realize this; he saw only the one spot where the track was rubbing against its mount. Determinedly he went off and returned with an oil can; he proceeded to douse the mount with oil. The squeak stopped, but then he realized that for some reason the next mount was squeaking, and so he moved along the deck and oiled that one, only to find that the next mount was squeaking also. He had reached the sixth track mount of perhaps a hundred, leaving half a dozen puddles of oil on deck, still trying to stop that pesky squeak and still unaware that every track mount on deck was squeaking, when the mate came upon him and explained the facts with some emphasis.

The builders of lake vessels have realized the flexibility of their ships and the need to use steel that has sufficient spring, ever since one of the earliest steel freighters, the *Western Reserve,* broke in two on Lake Superior during a summer storm in 1892, with the loss of all but one of her crew as well as of her owner, his wife and two children, his sister-in-law, and his niece. The ship was only two years old. It was concluded that the steel of which she was constructed was too brittle. Today the builders carefully determine the flexibility of the steel they use. But if the metal should become less flexible with age, or if the ship should meet a storm that twists her

*Lake freighter engineroom; this
particular ship is equipped
with steam turbines.*

beyond the limits of flexibility, disaster may result.

Some lakers can approach a speed of twenty miles per hour. (On the Lakes, speeds normally are given in statute miles per hour rather than in knots as on the ocean, though vessels that travel through the Seaway may use both systems.) A ship moving this fast produces a considerable wake, which in narrow waters rolls up on the shore with some violence. Therefore speed limits have been set by the Coast Guard in places where the wash from a ship might do damage, usually because summer cottages with docks and boathouses have been built along the shore. Two such places are on the upper reaches of the Saint Lawrence River and along the Saint Mary's River on the approaches below Sault Sainte Marie. In the latter area the limit is nine miles per hour.

Ship operators complain with some justice that they were there first; if people want to move into those areas and build docks and boathouses they should build them to meet existing conditions, not force the freighters to change their methods of operation. Some of the cottagers, they contend, simply hate ships; and they cite one elderly woman living on the Saint Mary's River who regularly telephones the Coast Guard to complain that every vessel passing is exceeding the limit. She even reported one ancient tub whose captain was much flattered to be told by the Coast Guard that he had been accused of going too fast; his vessel was incapable of moving at more than five miles per hour.

In open water the newer lakers can attain a good speed, but under the stringent government regulations that now prevail on both sides of the Lakes nothing so untoward as a race between ships would ever develop. A certain amount of mild dueling can sometimes be seen, however. If, for example, two ships are approaching a canal lock, the one that arrives first may save considerable time; the second comer not only will have to wait for the first one to go through but probably will have to wait for a vessel bound in the opposite direction to go through as well. Under these conditions there is a tendency for each captain to get as much speed out of his ship as he can. Slower vessels sometimes resort to psychological warfare at such times, calling the canal authorities or the Coast Guard to ask if there are speed limits in the area or whether passing is forbidden there — realizing full well that their faster competitors are listening on the same wavelength. Even though all concerned may know that the actions of an overtaking vessel are quite legal, such a call is apt to make her captain proceed more carefully.

All commercial vessels on the Lakes have radiotelephones through which they talk to shore stations and to each other. The days of professional wireless operators are long gone; now the officer on watch simply picks up a telephone handset, presses a button for the correct wavelength and speaks. Conversations between ships usually are friendly, although occasionally they may be like the comment from a large freighter in the Welland Canal on meeting a small one that insisted on hogging the middle of the channel despite whistle signals and polite radio requests to give way: "If you don't move over I'll move you over!" More often they are pleasant greetings between friends on different ships, which probably end as did one with the captain of the ill-fated *Daniel J. Morrell* on a day late in November, "Goodbye; talk to you Monday, Art." But, in that case, Monday never came for ship or captain.

In addition to the lakers, one sees on the Great Lakes several other kinds of freight vessels. There are tankers, which are much like their saltwater counterparts and which sometimes operate interchangeably in Great Lakes or ocean service. There also are two kinds of vessels unique to the Lakes — the railroad car ferries and the package freighters. The railroad car ferries originated on Lake Michigan and still operate there,

Railroad car ferry leaving Milwaukee harbor.

for that lake lies across the major east-west rail lines and there is considerable advantage in carrying rail cars directly across rather than sending them around through the Chicago complex. Of the several companies that operate such vessels, the Chesapeake and Ohio has the largest and most modern fleet, based at Ludington, Michigan. These vessels are built as icebreakers and operate throughout the winter. They load rail cars over their sterns, which then are closed off by sea gates — large metal gates that are lowered into place to keep following waves from coming aboard. The largest of these ships are about four hundred feet long.

Package freight is the term used on the Great Lakes for domestic general cargo. In the days when steamers were the fastest method of transportation between cities, nearly every passenger steamer carried package freight, so called to distinguish it from bulk freight. Then special package-freight ships evolved. On the American side of the Lakes, all this came to an end with the rise of the motor truck, but for a combination of reasons it has continued on the Canadian side. Canada Steamship Lines, the only company now operating such vessels, has a specialized package-freight service consisting of eight ships which average about 450 feet in length. The company also owns package-freight terminals in major Canadian cities on the Saint Lawrence and the Lakes and has as a subsidiary a trucking company that carries goods to and from the terminals. In addition, its vessels may call at American ports when it has cargo for them. For example, rolls of newsprint manufactured by paper mills at Thunder Bay are delivered regularly at Toledo by package freighter for use in most of the newspapers in northwestern Ohio. The modern package-freight ships have side ports through which their cargo is speedily loaded and unloaded directly from the dockside terminal.

Package freighter. These vessels are loaded and unloaded through side ports. This Canadian package freighter unloads newsprint from the paper mills of Thunder Bay for newspapers of northwestern Ohio.

Older, gravity-operated ore docks such as this one on Lake Superior are gradually being replaced by conveyor-belt loaders.

The major reason that these ships still can operate lies in Canadian geography. A glance at the map shows that the most heavily populated Canadian provinces, Ontario and Quebec, are strung out along the Saint Lawrence and the Lakes. It is obvious that a well-organized shipping line can carry manufactured goods from Montreal to Thunder Bay in larger — and thus less expensive — lots than can a trucking line, and yet probably be more flexible than a railroad. On the other hand it is obvious that between Cleveland and Chicago both trucks and rail lines are far more practical carriers of general freight than are ships. Also in favor of the Canadian operation is that CSL is a large and efficient organi-

zation, so much so that it even builds its ships in its own shipyards, thus reducing costs. The Canadian package-freight trade depends heavily on use of the Seaway; any lengthening of the Seaway season would undoubtedly bring it additional cargo.

Bulk freight, carried in lakers, is the predominant kind, however. Of the three most important lake trades, the carriage of ore is the main one. More ore moves over the Lakes than any other cargo. Next in importance is coal. Third comes grain. In the best of years, the amounts of grain moved are not as great as those of the other two leaders, and grain movements are more variable because they depend both on the yields of crops and the overseas markets for the grain. Each new generation of freighters sets new records carrying these cargoes. For many years the 633-foot Canadian freighter *Lemoyne,* launched in 1926, held almost every carrying record on the Lakes. Finally she made one last unhappy record: in 1969 she was towed to Europe to be scrapped, the newest and largest lake freighter yet to meet such an end. Her records by that time had been broken by ships whose records have in turn been superseded. The new generation of thousand-footers will now establish their own records.

Not only do the ships and cargoes get larger, but the navigational season gets longer. Traditionally, the season closed in early December and did not reopen until April. Now, however, there is pressure for more and more extended navigational seasons. A transportation system that is closed down for a quarter of the year is not only inefficient, but is also vulnerable to competition from the railroads, which are less efficient in other ways but can keep moving without serious difficulty throughout the winter.

United States Steel, which owns the largest fleet on the Lakes, set out in the winter of 1970-71, with the help of the Coast Guard and the Corps of Engineers, to operate as long as possible. For this experiment it used seven of its ships, which carried ore from Two Harbors, at the head of Lake Superior, to Chicago and Gary. On February 2, the last of them was laid up, to end a shipping season ten months long, the longest in history to that point. The canal gates at Sault Sainte Marie were kept free of ice by bubblers installed by the Corps of Engineers. These devices let air rise through the water and the bubbles keep ice from forming. The Coast Guard provided the icebreaker *Mackinaw,* the only U.S. government vessel designed primarily as an icebreaker then stationed on the Lakes. When it finally became evident that the *Mackinaw* was needed in two places — Whitefish Bay on Lake Superior and the Straits of Mackinac — at the

same time, the experiment was brought to an end; but it gave impetus to further efforts at gradually whittling away the closed season.

Prior to the winter of 1971-72, the U.S. Coast Guard brought the polar icebreaker *Edisto* into the Lakes, basing her at Milwaukee. During that winter the two big icebreakers worked together to keep the shipping lanes open, while ore freighters kept moving through sub-zero weather and winter storms. On February 3, 1972, the last two U.S. Steel vessels finished unloading their ore at South Chicago and headed for their winter berths at Milwaukee. At the same time the Coast Guard carried out "Operation Oil Can" — a program to keep ports open on the southeastern shore of Lake Michigan all winter long so that tankers could carry petroleum products into them, and "Operation Coal Shovel" — a program to keep the waterways open between Toledo, on western Lake Erie, and Detroit, so that freighters carrying coal could get through to the motor city.

One of the leading naval architects in the United States is Harry Benford, a lean, sharp-minded, graying man. He is a professor in the Department of Naval Architecture and Marine Engineering at the University of Michigan, the largest such department in the United States. Not long ago he was one of a group of experts on Great Lakes shipping who visited the Baltic to learn how nations there keep their waterborne commerce moving during the winter. It is ironic that at one time Europeans came to the Great Lakes to learn about ice-breaking techniques; now one Finnish shipyard has built over half the icebreakers in the world, and we go to the Baltic to learn how ships continue to move during the winter. Baltic governments in their taxing methods encourage construction of vessels that are reinforced for operation in ice; the U.S. government, as part of its recent interest in Great Lakes commerce, has begun to support research on the best types of ice reinforcement for lake vessels. Professor Benford looks forward to navigation on the Lakes for at least eleven months of the year and quite possibly twelve.

The larger the vessel, the less the cost per ton of moving a bulk cargo. Thus we not only will see the new thousand-footers, but probably a few even larger ships will emerge within the comparatively near future for use on runs where they do not need to go through canals. This will pressure government agencies to lengthen and especially to widen their canal locks. Marine technology is one of the most conservative of fields, but as a result of watching their fleets grow steadily more obsolescent in recent years, Lake shipping companies are acutely aware that they must innovate to stay alive. New methods of construction, new materials, and improved designs are in order.

To speak of mass producing thousand-foot ships is not quite accurate, but the factory techniques developed at the Erie shipyard of Litton Industries are as close to mass production methods as the product allows. We certainly will see more such operations around the Lakes as North American builders accept — and, one may hope, improve upon — the ideas of overseas builders. In the Great Lakes region the weather is less than comfortable for a number of months of the year; in such a region the desirability of building ships indoors is obvious. Both climate and economics favor the concept of ship factories. These factories will probably try to follow the lead of true mass production industries by offering a limited number of models but virtually unlimited variations within those models. Ships, like cars, can be provided with a range of available power plants, steering, and electrical equipment, installed to order in the same basic unit. All this of course will hold down construction costs.

After a time of stagnation, at least on the American side of the Lakes, we seem now to be entering a period of opportunity and growth. The U.S. government is finally giving its marine industries on the Lakes the same breaks it long has given those on salt water. Throughout increased shipping seasons we should before long have even bigger and more efficient lakers plying between our inland ports.

Last port. A vessel being scrapped. Small bulk freighters like this 500-footer can no longer compete in an era of 700- to 1,000-footers.

Toronto, on Lake Ontario, is a good example of a Great Lakes port. Here a lake freighter moves out of the western entrance to the harbor carefully picking her way through pleasure craft. In the background is the Hearn electric generating station.

3. harbors and shipyards

Lake ports vary widely in character. The small harbor at Conneaut receives iron ore and some limestone, and it ships coal; Thunder Bay at the Canadian Lakehead is the biggest grain-shipping port of them all; and fully half the tonnage through the port of Ludington is carried by those specialized Lake Michigan vessels, the railroad car ferries.

Domestic (U.S. and Canadian) trade is the solid foundation of harbor operations on the Lakes, but more ports are attracted by the glamor of overseas trade than can reasonably profit by it. For example, along Lake Erie's Ohio shore alone there are some half dozen harbors that receive ore and that may handle other bulk commodities in varying quantities. Each of these ports has grown up because it serves a specific domestic need; they compete only in the most general sense. But the two largest Ohio port cities, Cleveland and Toledo, which are only about one hundred miles apart, both aspire to be ports for ocean shipping. Both have developed suitable harbor facilities. In this trade the two ports compete directly; they draw on much the same territory. Few ocean ships will take the time to call at both, and shipowners may feel that neither port in itself offers enough cargo for a regularly scheduled stop. Thus it is likely that neither can provide the service that would be available at a single Ohio overseas port.

The biggest port on the Lakes is Chicago. Like other lake ports, it relies most heavily on domestic cargo, but makes great efforts to promote overseas trade. Navy Pier, on the city's waterfront, houses the port executive offices and handles some of the overseas shipping;

Cleveland harbor lighthouse.

but eleven miles south of the pier is Calumet Harbor, leading to Calumet River and Lake Calumet, and most of the port facilities are located on the shores of this complex. At the mouth of the river is the Transoceanic Terminal, and along its length are grain elevators and a rail-to-water transfer coal dock. Around Lake Calumet are storage points for almost any bulk cargo, dry or liquid. Lake Calumet is also the place at which cargoes can be transferred between lake or ocean freighters and river barges that ply the Illinois and Mississippi rivers and the other inland waterways.

By putting most of the commercial harbor facilities in the Calumet area, the city has gained the reputation among both lake and ocean seamen for having grimy, cramped, and generally uninspiring harbor environs. But it also has kept its main lakefront available for parks, marinas, and beaches, which most people prefer to docks, warehouses, and steel mills. All of this did not just happen; since 1909, Chicago has had a long-range development plan that it has followed with same care. The city also takes steps to control waterfront pollution, even to hoisting portable privies for the crews aboard freighters that do not have holding tanks for sewage.

Because of the great variety, it is hard to choose an average or representative Lake port. Perhaps the best one to ex-amine in some detail is the port of Toronto at the western end of Lake Ontario. It is neither as big as Chicago nor as specialized as many other ports. It serves both a large and growing metropolitan area and a highly industrial and thickly populated hinterland. The problems it faces are those of many ports, and the solutions it finds may be of use to others.

The Toronto harbor area, like that of most large ports, is controlled by several interlocking agencies. Those that control the fifty-mile waterfront of Metropolitan Toronto seem numerous and complicated, but they are considerably fewer than the thirty-four public bodies that held jurisdiction along that stretch of shoreline in 1939. The two most important municipalities today are Toronto proper and Metropolitan Toronto — the expanded political framework that ties the five surrounding boroughs and the city itself together, which has become the primary municipal government of the area. Both Toronto and Metro Toronto own island property in the harbor. The Province of Ontario owns the lake bed, but the federal government owns the bottom of the harbor.

The most important agency is the Toronto Harbor Commissioners, an administrative body headed by a general manager who carries out the policies of the five commissioners themselves. Despite its name it is a federal agency, although three of the commissioners are appointed by the city. As an example of the way in which government functions are interwoven, the Toronto Harbor Commissioners provide the police force of the Port of Toronto. The force is commanded by a veteran of the Metro Toronto police; the men are trained by the Province of Ontario, and they are then sworn in both as constables for the Port of Toronto and special constables for the Province of Ontario. The port police even have a detective branch, whose members can move anywhere in the province to investigate offenses that center on the port area and to make arrests if necessary.

Next most important agency is the Metro Toronto and Region Conservation Authority, the Ontario governmental arm that supervises landfill operations, erosion control, and major recreational activities along most of the waterfront. A third agency that may enter the picture is the Ontario body that eventually may build and supervise Harbor City, a development consisting of twenty thousand housing units planned for part of the island complex that forms the outer rim of the harbor. The Toronto Harbor Commissioners have worked out the plan, and the province (which provided much of the money for the planning) is solidly behind it. But the Metro Toronto government is less than enthusiastic and the

Harbors may be small and specialized, like this one at Conneaut, on Lake Erie. Here Hulett unloaders empty an ore carrier while a tug tows a self-unloader backward to the coal loading dock. Piles of crushed limestone are on the far pier. These are the three commodities the port handles.

project has not progressed with any speed — an example of the problems that arise from the divided control that affects most ports.

Despite such problems, this port appears to flourish. Along the waterfront are a number of piers, owned mostly by the Harbor Commissioners, where ocean freighters load and unload both general and bulk cargo. Toronto leads most Great Lakes ports in its ability to handle containers. There is a special container terminal owned by the Commissioners, which is equipped with cranes, lifters, and buildings designed for the purpose. One mobile crane alone cost six hundred thousand dollars. It was built in Germany especially for Toronto, and the builders have since received queries from overseas ports as well as from the ports of San Francisco and Port Everglades. A fifty-six-ton overhead lift truck to carry forty-foot containers cost one hundred seventy thousand dollars. As the first major port at the head of the Seaway, Toronto draws many ocean ships, some of which go no farther into the Lakes. Ships come not only from Europe, but also from the Far East, Australia, Latin America, the Mediterranean, and the U.S.S.R. In a typical year, cargoes arrive from about sixty countries and are shipped out to about the same number. In the harbor there also are privately owned grain elevators

that bring lake freighters, an oil storage area with docks for tankers, and the major Hearn Electric Generating Plant where self-unloading lake freighters deposit coal.

The Hearn plant, situated squarely on the harbor, has become a symbol of air pollution for some Torontonians and a headache for Ontario Hydro, the agency that owns and runs it. The Hearn plant is not new: work began on it in 1949, and it first went into operation in 1951. Its location, convenient at the time, is now an embarrassment. Hearn's chimneys, short by today's standards, pour out smoke and gases. As a result, the plant currently operates at only about 50 percent of its capacity, and its owners plan to phase it down to 25 percent of capacity. At the same time, they have built a new, high, nine-million-dollar chimney, which shoots the sulfur dioxide high into the atmosphere, away from Toronto; and they have converted a large part of the plant from using coal as fuel to using natural gas, which contains less sulfur.

One part of the future harbor plan that is going forward is the development of an outer harbor by the construction of a long arm of landfill to the southeast of the present harbor. When this is completed it will provide a basin almost as large as the natural harbor. Over a period of years the commercial docks will

Ship with containers as deck cargo, in Toronto harbor.

be moved to this area, releasing the present commercial waterfront for parks and other uses, somewhat after the Chicago pattern.

Meanwhile, however, Toronto manages to fit an amazing panorama of recreational activity into its harbor. On several of the islands there are parks and marinas, and on others, yacht clubs. The Royal Canadian Yacht Club, the granddaddy of Great Lakes yacht clubs, carefully maintains a large Victorian clubhouse among beautifully manicured lawns and gardens, and also carefully maintains an aura of Victorian country elegance that led one writer to say that the club launch ferried members "between the past of the club and the present of Toronto." Above all in recreational facilities is Ontario Place, a complex of modern buildings that reminds observers of a world's fair in microcosm, although it is a permanent fixture. Owned by the province, it stands along the shore just outside the western entrance to the harbor, built over a lagoon formed by carefully blocking off the lake with landfill to protect the buildings against the main sweep of waves. Ontario Place also incorporates a marina. As a result of all these boating facilities, the harbor on a summer day is full of pleasure craft; and the freighters may be observed picking their way carefully among them as they come and go.

In common with other ports, Toronto also has the problem of disposal of the sewage produced by the city — some 180 million gallons pass daily through its largest treatment plant, located at Ashbridge's Bay a little distance east of the harbor in a neighborhood that also houses a rendering plant. The odors from this area are normally carried eastward by the prevailing winds, away from the city but toward some of the neighboring communities, which do not always enjoy them. At times the problem is especially bad. During one two-week period, while technicians desperately tried to find the reason, the sewage treatment plant gave off the most horrid odors in recent memory. No one could discover why, until a chemist by chance remarked that it seemed as though all the bacteria were dead. Quickly the authorities checked, and they discovered that the billions of microscopic organisms that break down the sewage in such a plant were indeed dead. Further investigation showed that a local pharmaceutical company had dumped a bad batch of antibiotic pills down a drain; when the pills reached the ten acres of aeration tanks they functioned quite effectively, however, and destroyed all the bacteria there.

It is interesting to contrast the port of Toronto with that of Hamilton, another Ontario city an hour's auto (or truck) drive away. Normally two lake ports located so close together would injure each other's overseas trade by their competition, but that does not seem to happen here. The Toronto area houses mainly light industry and the cargoes that pass through the port reflect this. Hamilton, on the other hand, is the steel-manufacturing center of Canada. Its smaller port handles ore and the other incoming bulk products required by steel makers in the normal Great Lakes manner. Instead of installing container-handling equipment for ocean freighters, it has tried to specialize in cargoes that do not use containers, such as raw rubber and fertilizers.

A problem common to most Great Lakes harbors, whether at Hamilton or at Duluth, a thousand miles farther west, is that the fresh water of the Lakes and Seaway freezes during the winter months. One harbor official has commented that if the present closed season could be reduced even by a month on a regular basis, his ocean freight terminals would be kept busy the year around. The first steps toward keeping harbors open during freezing weather were taken at Duluth during the winter of 1970-71 and were so encouraging that they became the basis for developmental work under a $9.5 million program authorized by Congress.

Industrial water scene along the Cuyahoga River, a short distance upstream from the Cleveland harbor entrance.

Harbor lighthouse on the breakwater at Thunder Bay, on Lake Superior. The city can be seen across the harbor.

The large harbor that Duluth, Minnesota, shares with Superior, Wisconsin, handles ore, grain, and an assortment of other things including general cargo. Lake freighters carry ore and grain from here to other ports on the Lakes and Seaway; ocean freighters carry grain, perhaps scrap metal, and general cargoes overseas. It is the port not only for the bustling twin cities of Minneapolis and Saint Paul, 150 miles away, but also for an active six-state area in the upper Midwest. Some 45 million tons per year go through it, mostly outward bound. It is the westernmost harbor on the Lakes and one of the most northern. Minnesota is noted for its frigid winters, so

Duluth is a logical harbor to keep in operation as long as possible, for a system that keeps the ice open there should do the same at any other lake port.

The Duluth Port Authority began the project, getting financing from the Upper Great Lakes Regional Commission, the U.S. Maritime Administration, the U.S. Corps of Engineers, and the Saint Lawrence Seaway Development Corporation, to gather a total of fifty thousand dollars for the first test. Two parallel plastic pipes through which small holes were perforated were laid near the bottom of a main shipping channel; compressed air was then pumped through them. The rising air bubbles carried

Hamilton harbor, Lake Ontario. Two Russian seamen work at the bow of their freighter.

An empty ore carrier is being towed out of Lorain harbor
for a return trip to Lake Superior.

Tug station at Cleveland. The white building with a radio tower contains the dispatching office that sends tugs to assist vessels entering or leaving harbor.

warmer bottom water up to the ice, producing a strip of clear water thirty feet wide and reducing the thickness of surrounding ice from twenty-four inches to twelve inches, making it easy for a Coast Guard icebreaker to keep the channel clear. The success of this experiment led to installation of a bubbler system for use the following winter near Lime Island, along a bend in the Saint Mary's River — a major channel for shipping. At this point, the wakes of vessels making the sharp turn in winter weather have usually piled up ice that hindered following vessels. The bubblers considerably eased the problem.

Of all the industries that we traditionally associate with harbors, shipbuilding is the oldest. Often, however, the ports where shipyards are established do not possess the busiest commercial harbors. Lorain, Ohio, where the headquarters of the American Shipbuilding Company is located, is a steel mill city; but it is by no means a Cleveland or a Chicago. Erie, Pennsylvania, the home of Erie Marine, is a port of only moderate bustle. Collingwood, where the Collingwood Shipyards turn out many of the ships built on the Canadian side of the Lakes, has little else on its harbor but a shipyard.

People at the Davie Shipyard, located near Quebec and also owned by Canada

Steamship Lines, parent of the Collingwood yard, like to ask visitors from Collingwood if they are clearing the bush to make room for their new buildings or if the bears up there are troublesome. Although the Collingwood yard shares its harbor with only a grain elevator and a gaggle of fishing and pleasure boats, it scarcely is located in the wilderness as these jibes imply. Collingwood is as large as most of the other small cities on Georgian Bay. It has been a shipbuilding town since the late 1800s, and its shipyard has produced a steady stream of vessels that include many of the best under the Canadian flag.

The shipyard stands at the foot of the town's main street, and it is a bad year indeed when residents cannot glance down the street and see a big hull rising on the ways. There are a number of other enterprises in town, including a distillery that brings its grain in through that harbor elevator; but the shipyard employs the most men and is the heart of local industry. It also is an acknowledged leader in its own field. In addition to its construction facilities the yard has a design and engineering department that employs nearly one hundred people. It sells its patent winches to U.S. shipyards to install on their vessels, and its manager, W. A. Webster, has developed a rounded bow for ships that reduces water resistance in somewhat the

manner of the protruding bulbs used at the bows of some ocean-going vessels, but that unlike them does not take up valuable space in the locks through which the Great Lakes vessels must pass.

Traditional methods of building a steel ship from the keel up, piece by piece and plate by plate, have become so costly in recent years that most shipyards have abandoned them. Over the past twenty years the Collingwood yard has completely rearranged its procedures. Now the materials that go into the ship are unloaded in storage areas at one side of the yard, move through shops, furnaces, or working areas where they are processed, shaped, and put together under the roofs of large buildings. Then in the form of twenty-ton assemblies they are moved outside and lifted to the hull by big dockside cranes. Thus almost everything that makes up the ship is prefabricated before it is moved into place and fastened there.

The newest shipyard on the Great Lakes, that at Erie, carries the prefabrication idea even further. This yard, which built the first thousand-foot lake freighter, the *Stewart J. Cort*, manufactures entire segments of a ship's hull in a dockside factory, splices them together, and, as it adds the sections, pushes the ever-lengthening hull out-of-doors.

At the beginning of the process, steel

sheets from the yard's storage area enter one of the buildings, are shot-blasted to clean them and trimmed to exact size by automatic machinery, and then moving on rollers are carried through step after step where they are cut and welded together by machines that operate at the throw of a switch. The resulting sub-assemblies are moved by large trailers to the next building, where they are further assembled and then lifted by overhead traveling cranes into place on the segment of the ship — known as the module — that is being built at that moment. These segments are U-shaped cross-sections of the hull that are built lying flat. When completed they average six hundred tons in weight. As each one is ready it is moved ninety degrees into the vertical position by massive hydraulic machinery that tilts the entire bed on which the module was built and also powers a similar flat supporting surface that first rises against the module's side and then lowers that side slowly to its final position at the bottom of the ship.

The now upright U-shaped section then is welded to the part of the hull already constructed. As each module is added, the portion of the hull already completed is moved farther into the 1,250-foot drydock that is immediately outside the assembly building. (This is the largest drydock in the United States.) The procedure is the nearest thing to

THE AMERICAN SHIP BUILDING CO.

In the shipyard of the American Shipbuilding Company at Lorain, Ohio, lies the 858-foot laker *Roger Blough* shortly before her construction was completed. The picture catches two construction cranes forming an "A" above her.

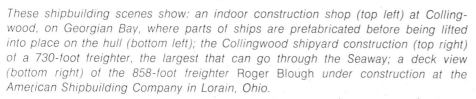

These shipbuilding scenes show: an indoor construction shop (top left) at Collingwood, on Georgian Bay, where parts of ships are prefabricated before being lifted into place on the hull (bottom left); the Collingwood shipyard construction (top right) of a 730-foot freighter, the largest that can go through the Seaway; a deck view (bottom right) of the 858-foot freighter Roger Blough under construction at the American Shipbuilding Company in Lorain, Ohio.

assembly line ship construction yet attempted in North America. It seems the best approach so far to keep rocketing shipbuilding costs somewhere within reason.

This hull factory at Erie does not build the bows and sterns of its ships. Bow and stern construction, at least to date, is not amenable to mass production; the ends of the vessels must be built in the older way and brought to the Erie facility.

Shipyards build the vessels, which then travel from port to port. But harbors also have a strong influence on ship design. For example, because of the winding Cuyahoga River at Cleveland, lakers delivering ore to steel mills on the upper river are limited in length to about 630 feet, and new vessels of that size are built to carry the ore. It will be some time before the thousand-footers take over in every trade.

Cleveland harbor, like many others, centers on the river, the Cuyahoga, that runs through it. Unfortunately, Cleveland's river has become notorious for its pollution, although it is equally well known to mariners for its many curves (*Cuyahoga* is variously translated from the Indian as meaning "crooked" or "snake," but the idea is the same in either case) and for its many bridges (twenty-five at last count). Many of the

Close-up of the bow of the first thousand-footer on the Lakes.
It is interesting to compare this picture with the view of the Blough (see pages 72 and 73). All of the same things are there, but they are arranged much differently.

bridges have to be lifted or drawn out of the way when a vessel passes; they usually move at their own good speed — slowly — while the waiting ship treads water until they get out of the way.

Navigating the inner reaches of Cleveland harbor thus calls for all of a lake captain's skill in maneuvering his vessel in close quarters. Little wonder that Cleveland has built its ocean freight terminal squarely on the waterfront so that the salties completely avoid the river. Ocean seamen are used to bigger waves and wider waters than those of the Lakes; but they don't always do well at sailing their ships through the eyes of needles.

The loading and unloading equipment provided at harbors has also long influenced lake vessel design, and still does. The *Cort,* the first thousand-footer, has smaller hatches than standard because she is intended to load only at ports such as Taconite Harbor on Lake Superior where pelletized ore is put aboard by conveyer systems. At the other end of the run, she can unload at harbors where her short unloading booms can reach suitable hoppers or other equipment designed to catch the ore they discharge.

Many ports today cannot accommodate thousand-footers, but throughout the history of lake shipping the builders have turned out increasingly bigger

The narrow, winding Cuyahoga River is the center of Cleveland harbor. A tug helps to guide a freighter around the bends in the river.

vessels and the ports have changed to fit them. The smaller ships will not disappear, for there are enough important harbors like Cleveland that absolutely require smaller vessels. In many places, however, harbor channels can be dredged deeper and wider, docks can be lengthened, and necessary equipment can be installed.

Milwaukee is one example of a port that probably could adjust rather easily to thousand-footers. The city has a large, protected outer harbor and an inner harbor that is not greatly restricted. In fact, part of the inner harbor is the municipal mooring basin, where as many as twenty of the 600-foot lakers anchor during the winter season for overhaul and repairs. The two harbors are separated by Jones Island (now actually a peninsula), on which is located many of the key terminal and rail facilities. On the opposite side of the inner harbor is a large grain elevator. The big freighters could not go far up any of the three rivers that lead out of the harbor; and so the river industries, like their counterparts in Cleveland, would still provide cargoes for smaller vessels. But if necessary — if, for example, the Seaway is eventually enlarged to allow the passage of thousand-footers — Milwaukee could no doubt ship cargoes in the large vessels without making great changes in its facilities.

Toronto waterfront. Great efforts are made to combine recreational use of the harbor with commercial use.

Cranes unloading heavy cargo, Milwaukee.

The port also is largely free of ice throughout the winter because the prevailing winds carry ice away from the western shore of the lake. Thus the harbor remains open to the rather limited winter shipping on Lake Michigan, but conditions elsewhere on the Lakes and the Seaway during the winter prevent other vessels from getting through. If the various agencies now working to extend the navigational season produce a good solution, they will find Milwaukee ready and waiting for it.

About six thousand vessels call there each year — an average of eighteen per day. They include ocean ships (there are some fifty overseas services), lakers, car ferries, tankers, and an assortment of other types; even Mississippi River barges are sometimes found in the harbor. Its publicists claim that in Milwaukee more diversified shipping can be seen than anywhere else on the Lakes, and that is easy for a visitor to believe. It seems likely that before many years there will be thousand-footers among the others.

We therefore may expect to see larger vessels in our ports; nevertheless there will still be many of moderate size for harbors and trades where the big ones do not fit. Self-unloading vessels seem to be the coming thing. More of them will no doubt appear, probably in newer and neater forms than those with the rather ungainly deck booms of the present. The *Cort,* which has short, retractable unloading booms that disappear into the superstructure, may be the pioneer in this regard as well as in many others. Over some time, as the result of this trend, dockside unloading machinery will change and dwindle, and some day even the Huletts may vanish from our harbors.

As ships grow larger they may also become fewer; one big ship can replace two small ones. There then may seem to be less harbor activity, even though an equal amount of cargo still moves. But as long as the big freighters come and go regularly, the ship-harbor combination will be doing its job, the ports will be economically healthy, and the inhabitants of the ports will have the particular esprit that an active harbor brings.

There is a special feeling about living in a harbor city, hearing the whistles of ships that come and go, and knowing that they connect the city with distant places. A port must have ships or it is no port. Whether in Buffalo, Milwaukee, or Duluth, the feeling is the same: when the whistles blow on leaving harbor one's spirit rises and wants to go along.

Indian ship in Milwaukee harbor; the Seaway makes Lake ports international.

Nuclear power plants take many shapes. This one is at Point Beach, Wisconsin, on Lake Michigan.

4. power

On the one hand, we have our technological civilization. Few people want to abandon it. Despite a scattering who retreat to communes and a larger number who talk about the return to a simpler life, it is hard to find anyone who really would like to go back to the medical care of fifty years ago, let alone the true simplicities of the Middle Ages. Despite the problems technology has brought us, it has in many ways been the force of freedom. There is difficulty in imagining women's liberation, for example, in a society devoid of electrical power and the pill. And ours is the first complex society that has not required support by a large class of people doomed to manual labor, whether they were legally free citizens or were serfs or slaves.

On the other hand, as technological man overflows the world he poses great threats to the ecology. In recent years we have just begun to realize some of the things we are doing. Most of them are lumped together under the term *pollution*, but there are others: strip mining, overlumbering, overfishing, irresponsible use of resources in many ways. Technology uncontrolled does tremendous damage. Mankind usually has cared more about the immediate gain than about the long-term disaster. It is handy but unfair to blame this on managers, politicians, scientists, or engineers; they have merely reflected the priorities we all have helped to form. The citizen who votes against taxes for building a new sewage disposal plant, the stockholder who objects to money spent for smoke abatement, and the man who throws his beer cans on the shores are the real villains — and they are all of us.

On a gray autumn day at Ashtabula, Ohio, self-unloading lake freighters take on coal. The small self-unloader at left is at the coal dock, loading; the larger one at right approaches it. These vessels carry the coal to power plants throughout the Great Lakes region and unload it directly at the plants.

Thus we have an apparent conflict between our technological and ecological needs. Perhaps our greatest problem today is somehow to gear these two sets of needs so that they work together rather than in opposition. Few activities are more completely involved with this problem than is the production of electrical power.

The manufacture of electricity demonstrates a conflict that all manufacturers face. On the one side there is a growing demand for the product. For example, electric power use has increased by 130 percent every ten years in the Urban Detroit Area, a convenient cross-section of the Great Lakes industrial region that includes nine Ohio counties and three Ontario counties as well as twenty-five Michigan counties. On the other side there is a growing concern for what the manufacturing process does to the environment. With power, the problem is more obvious and more direct than with most other manufactures. Conceivably we could do without the products of mills and factories, but it is hard to imagine contemporary life without electricity. Thus the difficulties that face the power companies are the basic problems of any industrial organization and its environment, but they go beyond that. One ecological writer, Jane Stein, in *Smithsonian*, the Institution's magazine, calls the conflict between the demands for energy and the demands for a sound environment "the central environmental issue the nation faces."

Power executives can at times be forgiven for deciding that they will never succeed in reconciling the conflict. The Niagara Mohawk Power Corporation was approached by a group of citizens who were annoyed because its tower headquarters in Buffalo was topped by fifty-six 1,000-watt lights, which had served as a nighttime decoration for the past sixty years. Turn them off, the group demanded; that act would be a symbol of a commitment to conserve energy. The company, knowing well how the environmental winds were blowing, turned off the lights. No sooner done than opposing civic groups raised a cry that the city had lost a historical landmark. After some two weeks of controversy the company, no doubt heaving a corporate sigh, decided that more people wanted the lights on than off, and so it illuminated its tower again.

Electricity usually is produced by converting water power, steam power, or (to a much lesser degree) internal combustion power. Electricity provides a convenient way of piping that power throughout our living areas and a flexible way of using it once it is delivered. In our homes it drives most of the devices that have replaced the servants of affluent housewives and the sweat of less-affluent ones; it provides light; and it powers those mixed blessings, radio and television. Through separate channels it brings energy to the telephone. It heats and cools. It drives the machinery of commercial plants ranging from small repair shops to major factories. In rural areas it runs water pumps and milking machines; in cities it drives both subways and elevators. When electricity fails, life as we know it stops.

Throughout the Great Lakes area there are various kinds of power stations to

Power lines span most tributaries of the Great Lakes; here two sets of lines cross the Severn River, just southeast of Georgian Bay.

change the various forms of energy into electricity that is fed into the delivery network. Hydroelectric stations are perhaps most typical of the Lakes region. Towers support high-voltage lines that festoon the banks of the fast running Niagara River and march away carrying power in all directions. Power dams on the Saint Lawrence River serve both the United States and Canada. Tributary rivers, especially those north of the border, help generate power. Hydroelectric generating stations do not pollute. They may do some harm to the environment in other ways, but with care even that can be minimized. The parklike Canadian side of the Niagara River shows that power production need not blight its environs. In the Province of Ontario, nearly half of all power comes from hydroelectric stations. The very name of the basic power agency there, Ontario Hydro, suggests that historically the Canadian side of the Lakes has looked to water power for generating its electricity.

But in Michigan, the central state on the American side of the Great Lakes, less than 5 percent of the electricity comes from hydroelectric plants. The main source in Michigan and what is

Coal dock and oil tanker. Coal and oil are two common sources used in the manufacture of electrical power.

just becoming the largest source in Ontario is steam power. (The first year in which thermal-electric power exceeded hydroelectric power in Ontario was 1970.) The fuel for most steam plants is coal; for some it is oil or fuel gas; and for a few it is nuclear material. The traditional powerhouse with its tall chimneys is still a major symbol of electrical production and it probably will remain so for a few years to come.

All those tall chimneys produce smoke. The smoke contains dirt, otherwise known as soot, fly ash, or particulate emission, which can be removed quite efficiently by electrostatic equipment that is about 98 percent effective. But the smoke also contains other things. Unless the coal or oil used as fuel is of the comparatively rare low sulfur variety, there will be sulfur dioxide, a gaseous, irritating form of the chemical that causes respiratory and possibly other illnesses. So far no one has developed a good way of getting rid of it. Numerous experiments are under way to develop methods of controlling sulfur dioxide; meanwhile the builders of power stations must content themselves with very high chimneys that shoot the stuff into the upper air where it is dissipated — except when there is a temperature inversion that holds it down.

Sometimes power companies put their stations on the windward shore of a lake, so that prevailing winds carry the smoke out over the water, thus avoiding heavily populated areas. But in this procedure there may be hidden traps. One of the other poisonous elements found in most fuel is selenium, and as a result small quantities of it are often present in smoke. Investigations of those areas of Lake Michigan over which smoke blows from Chicago and Milwaukee have shown that the minute animals in the water contain selenium in concentrations that may be dangerous to man. These animals are eaten by fish, but as yet we do not know if the fish retain the poison. This could be as dangerous a kind of pollution as that caused by mercury, although there also is some evidence that when *both* selenium and mercury are present in the flesh of ocean fish, the chemicals tend to combine into a form less readily absorbed by humans, and thus to cancel out the poisonous effects.

One answer to air pollution by power plants is the use of nuclear fuels. Properly constructed nuclear power stations cause little radiation danger, and they produce no smoke to contain harmful gases. Such power plants are clean; they have no coal dust to blow into the air or wash into the water as do so many of the current plants, which can hardly fail to pollute their immediate surroundings merely from their storage piles. The great difficulty is that a nuclear plant,

Hearn power station, Toronto.

Large hydroelectric station that harnesses the power of the Saint Lawrence River at Beauharnois.

ter *a minute*. Thus it solves the air pollution problem at the cost of adding to that relatively unknown quantity, thermal pollution.

Steam power systems require a constant flow of water for cooling. This is why we find them located beside bodies of water. Other industries use some water for the same purpose, but 80 percent of the cooling water drawn from lakes and rivers is used by electrical power plants. The water drawn out by a steam plant is discharged again at an average temperature twenty degrees higher than before. The amount of water so heated of course depends on the size of the power plant, and the impact on the body of water depends on its size. The effect of a single power plant upon a Great Lake or one of the major connecting rivers such as the Saint Clair cannot be measured. There is of course a considerable rise in temperature at the point where warm water flows back in, but as one moves farther away this quickly diminishes. Numbers of such plants, however, would raise the overall temperature of the lake or river. The U.S. Atomic Energy Commission's director of environmental affairs, Joseph Di Nunno, made the point, "Ten plants on the same lake or river may not hurt you. Eleven may not. But somewhere you'll put in just one more plant and you'll get pushed over the edge."

mainly for safety reasons, operates at lower steam pressures than plants using other fuels; it also has no chimneys to discharge heat into the air. Therefore it gives off into the water half again as much heat as a coal fired or oil fired plant of the same capacity. A thousand megawatt nuclear plant — one of the larger ones now under construction — will use 850,000 gallons of cooling wa-

Thermal pollution — damage to a body of water by adding heat — is one of the many areas in which our problems have outrun our knowledge. We know that too much heat will do harm. Warm water tends to stimulate the growth of unnecessary plant life, to attract less desirable kinds of fish such as carp, and to drive off or destroy some of the more valuable kinds. But we have no formulas to tell us how many power plants of a given size can be put into operation before they will change the water temperature of a specified lake, and we do not know how great a change there can be in overall temperature of a lake before disaster falls. Experiments now being conducted suggest that the dangers may not be as great as some people have felt, but we still are largely in the dark.

Despite the problems, nuclear fuel seems to be the coming thing. By the year 2000 there surely will be many nuclear generating plants located on the Great Lakes. In Ontario, where coal must be imported but fissionable material is a natural resource, they are beginning an extensive program to build nuclear stations. In the United States at present there is not as great a trend to nuclear power, but a number of such stations have been constructed. The mounting problems in obtaining the fossil fuels, coal and oil, particularly in sulfur-free varieties, are beginning to make nuclear fuel look more attractive.

John Noble Wilford, reporting in the *New York Times,* points out that "now, when thoughtful people close to the [power] issue talk about solutions, they almost unanimously fall back on nuclear energy as the only satisfactory way to accommodate society's needs and keep the traditional energy distribution system intact." But groups of environmental-minded citizens do not always see it that way, even though they may have no other solutions in mind. Often they just set out to block the construction of new plants. According to one harassed utility vice-president, "The number of objectors is mushrooming, and their demands are constantly increasing. They have no responsibility for meeting the nation's growing power requirements and no rational answer to their own power needs. Each group is essentially saying, 'Build your plant somewhere else.'"

Frustrating as all this is to those who do have the responsibility, and frivolous as the objections can become, it does insure that the siting of new power stations is given the most careful thought. One utility in a Great Lakes state even invited the environmental groups to take part in the decision-making process, and found that after the critics' first tendency to make speeches during meetings had subsided they would actually accept some responsibility. The Northern States Power Company was considering four sites for a new plant in Minnesota. Representatives of about thirty concerned groups were asked to join the task force that was choosing the new location. The body rejected the company's first choice out of hand because it was being considered as a state park, ruled out two others because there already were other plants nearby, and chose the fourth, which was the least desirable economically. The company accepted that location.

There are about twenty nuclear power plants either planned, under construction, or completed on the shores of the Great Lakes. The largest concentration, seven, is on Lake Michigan. In addition, there are twenty other power plants on that one lake. Fish and Wildlife Service experts calculated that over the next thirty years the heat discharged into the lake from all these plants would increase ten times. Clearly that would cause disaster. At first the Federal Water Quality Administration clamped severe restrictions on further dumping of heated water into the lake. Three of the four states around Lake Michigan quickly followed up by setting standards forbidding the discharge of any water that would raise the lake temperature over three degrees at an arc drawn one

thousand feet from the discharge point. The fourth state, Illinois, simply refused to permit new nuclear plants to be built on its part of the lakeshore.

One Lake Michigan plant, the Palisades station in southern Michigan, was attacked by a public action group that held up its opening by lawsuits while they argued with the company about both its supposed leakage of nuclear wastes into the water and its thermal discharges. The fight went on for nine months, while the company — and ultimately of course the power consumer — lost $105,000 each day the plant remained shut down. Finally Consumers Power Company agreed to impose more rigorous waste controls and to build cooling towers for the heated water.

The cooling tower is apparently the coming thing. In order to meet that three-degree restriction, all power plants on Lake Michigan must improve their cooling systems. Similar restrictions

Palisades nuclear power plant, on Lake Michigan. A public-action group forced this plant to remain closed until its owners built a cooling tower to prevent hot water from draining into the Lake.

Many of the new power plants being built on the Lakes use nuclear fuel. Here is one under construction on Lake Erie, near Toledo.

Base of a cooling tower under construction at the nuclear power plant on Lake Erie, near Toledo; when completed the power will rise four to five times the height shown here.

have been applied elsewhere on the Lakes. Construction of the Locust Point, Ohio plant near Toledo on Lake Erie, for example, was held up until its owners agreed to use cooling towers. There are various other cooling schemes, most of which have disadvantages; the cooling tower seems the best answer we have today. It is a squat concrete structure that may be as much as five hundred feet tall and three hundred feet in diameter at the base, tapering slightly as it rises and then flaring again at the top. Heated water from the plant is pumped into the tower and dripped over a lattice framework; air enters at the bottom, is warmed by the hot water, and rises through the tower, cooling the water by evaporation. In a variation of this scheme, fans draw the cooling air through the tower. The cooled water settles to the bottom and is either discharged into the lake or stream or is reused by the plant.

Cooling towers also add expense. Consumers Power Company, in agreeing to build towers and additional radioactive waste controls at the Palisades plant, estimated that the added construction would cost an extra $15 million and the added operational expenses would be $3 million a year. Once again the consumer will pay more for his electricity. It is easy to delude ourselves in such matters that we are on one side and industry is on the other, but the fact is that if we want a decent environment we are the people who in the long run will pay for it.

The cooling towers give off huge plumes of steam; a tower for a one-million-kilowatt plant throws out twenty to twenty-five thousand gallons of water each minute in the form of vapor. Predictably, the towers themselves have come under attack as environmental hazards. Will they not produce fog and ice? The project engineer for one plant that was being equipped with the expensive towers had a wry answer. "For some reason natural towers do not create significant fog, even though the law of physics indicates they should. I wish I could say otherwise." U.S. federal authorities agree that the effect from towers is limited and that it only reinforces such natural developments as the normal formation of cumulous clouds. As environmentalist Jane Stein writes, however, "One must wonder what cumulative meteorological effects would result when 30 years hence, thousands of towers were cooling the equivalent of one-third of the nation's fresh runoff, and ejecting vast quantities of heat and evaporated water into the air."

One answer is the dry tower, an example of which has been built in England. In it the water remains in something like a giant auto radiator while the

Hydroelectric plant at Severn Falls. At left is a marine railway that carries pleasure craft up and down past the falls.

cooling air passes through it; no water escapes. Such towers cost two and a half times as much as wet towers. Other answers still require more development. Theoretically it is possible to generate electricity more efficiently by different means, converting either fossil fuels or nuclear fuels directly into energy without using steam power and generators; but so far little emphasis has been put on their research.

Despite the furor about thermal pollution that has been raised in the United States, Ontario Hydro does not foresee the need for cooling towers at its nuclear plants on the Great Lakes. Ray Effer, a biologist in the employ of that organization, compares the output of heat into a Great Lake by a single nuclear plant over a whole year to the amount absorbed by the lake during half a day of sunshine. A publicity booklet put out by Hydro quotes U.S. sources that call cooling towers unsightly, and adds, "However, if Ontario Hydro had to locate a thermal plant on a small inland stream or lake, cooling towers or a cooling pond would probably be necessary." There is a certain defensive tone here, as though the dignified organization was glancing nervously over its shoulder at what is happening on the other side of the Lakes; but also there is obviously a different policy in Ontario. Why should this be?

Typical conventional power plant on the Michigan shore of the Saint Clair River.

Kewaunee nuclear power plant.

First, of course, Ontario has no such concentration of plants on one lake as that which threatened Lake Michigan. It has two nuclear plants operating or planned near Toronto on Lake Ontario and two others on Lake Huron—a large, cool, deep body of water which has relatively little industry on its shores. Its major expansion plans seem to involve the area on Lake Huron which it has dubbed "the nuclear capital of Canada." Surely the current rather small Douglas Point nuclear power station, which produces two hundred thousand kilowatts of electricity, does little harm to the lake. But the planned Bruce Generating Station, which is being constructed nearby, will consist of four units, each of which will produce four times as much as the Douglas Point station. Thus the Bruce station will have sixteen times the capacity of Douglas Point. At this juncture no one can really say what its thermal output will do to the lake.

Another factor is the differing public attitudes toward nuclear energy in the two countries. There is a vocal group in the United States that seems to have assumed a deep feeling of guilt because nuclear power even exists. As a result it feels that the evil genie, whatever its application, must be policed with the utmost care. It follows that nuclear generating stations are to be watched with great suspicion and placed under the

Some big new conventional plants still are being built. This is Ontario Hydro's Nanticoke Power Station under construction on the northern shore of Lake Erie.

most stringent controls. This group also feels, certainly with some justification, that neither government nor industry are always to be trusted when they make soothing assurances that all is well.

By contrast, most Canadians who think about such things seem to be rather proud of their country's sizable contribution to nuclear development. Their growing national consciousness also makes them both pleased that they own a large part of the world supply of fissionable material and determined to put it to use. Further, Canadians differ from Americans in that they are inclined to put fairly good people in those public jobs that are not directly political and to trust them to do fairly good work. Thus when an American power company says that no cooling towers are needed, the American intellectual community automatically rises in arms to force it to build cooling towers; but when Ontario Hydro says that no cooling towers are needed the Canadian intellectual community feels that its experts probably know what they are talking about.

It is dangerous to lean too heavily on such national comparisons, especially as public attitudes have a way of overflowing national boundaries. Pressure may one day force Ontario Hydro to build cooling towers at its nuclear plants. For that matter, its own scientists and engineers may decide that something of

Modern power pole, clouds, and sun.

the sort is necessary even if it is not a matter of public concern. But the fact remains that they have not been rushed willy-nilly into the construction of cooling towers as have their American counterparts.

All of the detailed problems surrounding power lead to a basic question, put concisely by writer Wilford in his *New York Times* report: "Is it possible to have a thriving, motorized, computerized, air-conditioned society with a high standard of living shared by as many as possible and a largely uncontrolled economy — and to have a comfortable, even beautiful, environment too?" It is not an easy question to answer, both because it requires much study that has not yet been done and because it may threaten some of our most dearly held preconceptions. Must we forget our ideal of an air conditioner in every home? Must we slow down our use of natural resources in order to preserve ourselves? If we do, what happens to the North American economy, which has been expanding vigorously for some two hundred years? And what will be the impact on the world economy? Could we survive better if we went to tightly planned national systems, with all of the philosophical and political implications that step involves? If we did so, what would be the psychological effects upon us? Neither the ba-

Is this pollution? Hot water from a nearby coal-fired power plant flows into Erie Bay at Erie, Pennsylvania, immediately under the replica of Commodore Perry's flagship at the Battle of Lake Erie, the U.S. Brig Niagara.

Douglas Point, Ontario, nuclear power station on Lake Huron.

sic question nor the secondary ones are likely to be answered in the near future, but they are questions that must be asked.

The factor that probably will exercise the most immediate control is cost. The charges made for electricity are usually regulated by government agencies, and so the normal supply-and-demand relationship is somewhat dampened. It must prevail finally, however. Utility companies complain that their current profit margins make it hard for them to borrow money for development and expansion. A number of people have suggested that energy prices should cover "the full cost to society" — in other words, the costs of preventing air and water pollution as well as the other costs. To some extent that is automatic: when a utility builds cooling towers it must add proportionately to what it charges its customers. But many other such costs are underwritten by taxes that have little relationship to power consumption. It would seem to make sense, for example, to charge part of the government's cost of monitoring pollution directly to the utilities, and for them to charge their customers accordingly. Whatever the schemes that are worked out, it is likely that the cost of power will be one control upon its use.

The many pressures should speed up development of the now largely theoretical ways of getting electricity from fuel in neater, more efficient manners. One system, with the jaw-twisting name *magnetohydrodynamics* (abbreviated MHD), converts either nuclear or fossil fuels almost directly to electricity at some 60 percent efficiency, as compared to 30 percent for present nuclear plants. The other, nuclear fusion, may offer 90 percent efficiency without any thermal wastes. Both of these, however, are more likely processes for the year 2000 than for the near future. Harold A. Smith, chief engineer for Ontario Hydro, expects his organization to have a small prototype MHD plant working the last decade of this century.

Until the year 2000 it appears that we can expect more of what we are now having: conflicts between environmentalists and utilities, cooling towers, and rising costs. There may even be rationing at certain times and places. During the intervening years some of the problems surely will sort themselves out. But the process will not be easy and often it will not be pleasant.

Power towers crossing Sandusky Bay, Lake Erie.

Fishing boat on Lake Superior at Marquette, Michigan.

5. fishes and fisheries

At Wheatley, Ontario, on the northwestern shore of Lake Erie, the steel fishing tugs come into the small harbor through a narrow entrance between two long jetties. When a quartering breeze kicks up a chop on the lake, the seventy-footers move with a roll and a wallow. They are clumsy looking craft with long, high superstructures; but their captains are skillful helmsmen. They pass through the entrance with casual precision. Once inside the harbor, the skippers steer over to the dock of what reputedly is the largest freshwater fish-packing plant in the world, and there unload their catches.

These days the best they bring are yellow perch and white bass of modest size, piled with crushed ice in the wooden fish boxes. The crewmen stack the boxes half-a-dozen high; then men with forklifts pick up whole stacks at a time and, running their machines backward, carry the loads into the plant. There in an assembly-line process fish are sorted for size, washed, and scaled. Their heads and tails are removed. All of this is done by semiautomatic machinery. A conveyer belt then delivers the fish to the filleting tables, where women cut each fish into two boneless sticks and discard the waste. The sticks are breaded, then moved by other conveyer belts through an infrared oven to automatic packaging machinery and thence to a quick freezer. This same procedure, with minor variations and simplifications, is also performed at smaller plants along the northern Erie shore. About half of the fish taken in the Great Lakes today come from Lake Erie and at least three-quarters of the Lake Erie fish are taken on the Canadian side — al-

Gulls follow a trawler on Lake Erie.

though some 95 percent of the Canadian catch eventually goes in refrigerated trucks or rail cars to cities of the United States.

Smaller quantities of larger fish of the preferred species, usually taken from one of the other Great Lakes, are still sent whole or dressed to market. But the general decline in size and kind of lake fish and the rise in popularity of processed frozen foods have led to dockside plants that convert fish of moderate desirability into acceptable foodstuff.

For many years, Great Lakes fisheries have been in a state of chaos. Statistics can be misleading; for example, in both 1897 and 1968, roughly 116 million pounds of fish were taken from the Lakes. It might seem that the fisheries maintained amazing stability over a period of seventy-odd years. But in 1897 the greatest single variety caught was herring; others taken in some numbers were whitefish, lake trout, walleye, and yellow perch. The perch were not considered very good fish. In 1968 there still were a number of perch — now the best of those taken — and much of the catch was made up of smelt, carp, and various other creatures ranging from channel cat to alewife. Only in Lake Superior was herring still a major catch. Throughout the Lakes today we have the results of a series of biological disasters. As one expert, Stanford H. Smith, puts it, the fish

stocks of the Great Lakes "have been outstanding examples of abuse although they are the world's largest and most valuable freshwater fishery resource."

Man's impact on lake fish began early. As settlement moved westward in postcolonial days, Lake Ontario was the first of the chain to support commercial fishing. At that time the Atlantic salmon abounded in the lake and was much prized, but it began to decline after 1835 and by 1890 was extinct. Its disappearance was apparently caused as much by destruction of its spawning grounds as by overfishing. To spawn, the salmon swam up the various streams draining into the lake. But settlement brought mill dams, the cutting down of forests, and disposal of wastes into the water. The flow of the streams was reduced, the quality of the water fell, and probably the temperature of it rose. The salmon no longer could reproduce.

From the mid-1800s to the mid-1900s the technology of fishing developed about as rapidly as all the other technologies of the world. On the Lakes the fleets of relatively small sailing fish boats came at first to be assisted by steam tugs, which could tow them to the fishing grounds and then take the catch to market as quickly as possible. Soon the tugs themselves were outfitted with fishing gear and gradually replaced the sailboats. They grew larger and were equipped with improved devices such as powered net-lifters. Bulky steam engines were replaced by compact diesels. Turtleback cabins covered the decks to give sheltered working space. (Although the character of the boats had completely changed, they still were called tugs.) Net materials changed over the years from linen (which first was obtained, according to a story, by the fishermen's womenfolk unraveling their old garments) to cotton to nylon. With each new development, fewer men caught more fish.

Some species were destroyed intentionally. The lake sturgeon was one large fish that was common in every Great Lake during the 1800s. It was not particularly valuable, and because of its size it damaged fishing gear. To commercial fishermen it was a big, blundering nuisance, and they set out to get rid of it. In the late 1800s the catches of sturgeon in each of the major Lakes exceeded a million pounds a year — and these figures do not include the uncounted numbers that were simply killed and not marketed. Old residents of lake fishing ports recall seeing sturgeon piled up on the beaches like cordwood, doused with kerosene, and burned. By the 1920s sturgeon were so scarce that in most U.S. waters they were legally protected. Today a small population of them barely holds its own.

Fish dock at Cleveland, Ohio.

At Wheatley, Ontario, on Lake Erie,
fishing gear is piled in front
of a typical fishing boat.

Commercial fishery at Port Dover,
on the Canadian side of Lake Erie.

*One man shovels smelt into the box while another brings
crushed ice from a dockside plant.*

Throughout the 1800s and early 1900s, herring (known popularly as "cisco" along the Lakes) was a common and valuable fish, often making up a third of the total quantity caught. The herring of Lake Erie were especially large and plentiful. Markets were available in both Great Lakes and eastern cities. The recorded catches in some years reached nearly fifty million pounds; probably the actual catches were even greater. In 1924 over thirty-two million pounds of herring were caught in Lake Erie; the next year only about six million pounds were caught; the next the figure dropped to about three million; by 1930 it was less than one million. There were other causes for this decline — the herring seems to have been particularly sensitive to pollution — but a major one simply was overfishing.

These are examples of what man has done directly to fish in the Great Lakes. Indirectly he also has released destructive forces. Perhaps most striking is the impact of what scientists call "exotic species" — species that originated outside the Lakes. The most efficient and least pleasant of these aliens is the sea lamprey, an eellike creature that may attain a length of over two feet. It has a round, sucking mouth reminiscent of a small vacuum cleaner fitted with many teeth, and a sharp, rasping tongue. It

hunts large fish, attaches itself to one of them by its mouth, and with its sharp tongue rasps a hole in the fish's side through which it drains its victim's juices. Lampreys may kill their prey or may leave them weakened and subject to infection or attack by other predators.

In North America, lampreys today are not considered edible, though in other times and places they were thought of as delicacies. King Henry I of England died from "a surfeit of lampreys." Indians along the Atlantic Coast fished for them, and New Englanders until comparatively recent times ate them with pleasure. Today we do not even use them for bait, as the Dutch once did. Aboard Dutch fishing vessels a small boy was assigned the interesting job of making them easier to handle by biting off their heads.

Sea lampreys have existed in Lake Ontario at least since the 1880s, probably arriving there from the ocean by way of the Saint Lawrence River. Persistent animals, the lampreys also reached the Finger Lakes of New York via the Erie Canal from the Hudson; and some theorists believe that they moved into Lake Ontario from those lakes. In any event, the sea lamprey is undoubtedly the reason that large fish have been scarce in Lake Ontario since the extinction of the Atlantic salmon.

Niagara Falls kept fish from moving upriver to Lake Erie just as effectively as

Fishboxes already filled with smelt are lifted by block and tackle so that a forklift can pick them up and carry them into a processing plant.

Fish, fishermen, and fishing boats at Wheatley, Lake Erie.

Fishing port of Killarney, Georgian Bay.

it prevented ships from doing the same thing. In 1829, the first Welland Canal was opened to let vessels pass between Lakes Ontario and Erie. In time the sea lamprey also discovered the canal; the first one was found in Lake Erie in 1921. Shallow, warm Lake Erie, with few spawning streams, offered the repulsive creature little comfort. But by 1932 it was established in Lake Huron, by 1936 in Lake Michigan, and by 1946 in Lake Superior. It attacked the large fish in the upper Lakes, almost completely destroying the lake trout, seriously depleting whitefish, walleye, and other species, and establishing itself as the dominant form of marine life.

Because the larger predators had been so depleted by the sea lamprey, the smaller species multiplied and grew in size, at times to the point that the lamprey attacked some of them as well. By wiping out the larger fish, the lamprey invasion also opened the way for another exotic fish to enter the upper Lakes. This was the alewife, a small saltwater fish that flourished as the lamprey killed off the big species that otherwise would have controlled it.

The alewife had also reached Lake Ontario by the 1860s. Theories vary, but quite probably it came by way of the Erie Canal. In freshwater, this ocean fish rarely grows longer than eight

Setting gill nets (left), Georgian Bay. The nets are doused with soapy water to keep them slippery so they do not tangle, and to help keep them clean. As the boat moves ahead slowly, the nets are paid out over the stern. Raising gill nets (below). A fish is in the net just being brought in by the power net lifter, at right.

inches. Its only value when caught is for pet food or fertilizer. Because the sea lamprey had cleared away the large predators, the alewife by 1880 was the most abundant fish in Lake Ontario. It followed close behind the lamprey into the upper Lakes and there, with no predators to control it, competed so vigorously with the other small species that it nearly annihilated them. In Lake Michigan, for example, in 1960 only 8 percent of the fish caught in experimental trawls were alewives; by 1966 80 percent of such catches were made up of these fish. Not only is the alewife a worthless creature that has driven out good ones, but it has the further unpleasant habit of periodically dying in great schools that subsequently defile beaches and clog water intakes. These deaths have not been fully explained, but evidently what is basically a saltwater fish sometimes meets conditions in freshwater that it cannot withstand.

In a number of places man also has changed conditions drastically by his various kinds of pollution. This is particularly true in shallow areas such as the western end of Lake Erie and Green Bay of Lake Michigan, areas where fishing in the past has been particularly good. Solids of various kinds, produced by humans and dissolved in the water, have increased greatly over the past cen-

tury. These change the chemical content of the water and provide such potent fertilizers that algae grow abundantly, then die abundantly, and rot abundantly, using up the dissolved oxygen in the water. Herring and whitefish apparently cannot live in such areas. From the 1870s to the 1920s the catches of these fish began to decline first in the Detroit River, then in western Lake Erie, and finally they disappeared throughout the entire lake. These are the areas, as we know now, that of all the Lakes have been the most polluted. The eggs of nearly all Great Lakes fish settle to the bottom; the changes in bottom sediments may well affect them. As the population around Lake Erie and the Detroit River has grown, man has dumped so many different things into them that it is not possible to say what all the effects may be on marine life; but it is obvious that they are great. Lake Erie has been the least affected of the Lakes by either the sea lamprey or the alewife, but it has had the greatest pollution. Such worthless forms as sheepshead now flourish in Erie. Fishermen and scientists wonder if the valuable walleye and yellow perch, which require fairly clean water, may follow the herring and whitefish into oblivion.

Recently we have become aware of a completely different sort of pollution, one that does not injure the fish in the

Net buoys, leaning against a fish house at Bayfield, on Lake Huron. Fishermen indicate the positions of their nets by these buoys, which float on the surface above them. Each buoy is marked to show who is the owner of the nets.

Nets drying at Port Dover.

Lakes but that could be fatal to human beings who eat them. It is pollution by mercury. The major sources of it have been industrial plants that drained supposedly inert mercury waste into the water. Now it is evident that the mercury does not remain inert, but through a complex process enters the food chain and eventually comes into the body of the fish. Health authorities say that fish containing more than one-half part of mercury per million should not be eaten. Fish in the Saint Clair River–Lake Saint Clair–Detroit River complex are so thoroughly saturated with mercury that the commercial fisheries there have been closed. The mercury has washed into western Lake Erie, and fisheries there have also been closed or limited. The small fisheries in eastern Lake Ontario and the upper Saint Lawrence have been closed because of industrial drainage of mercury from inland New York State. Although strict controls have been put on the release of mercury into the water by factories, large amounts remain on the bottom and continue to be absorbed by the fish. No one knows just how long it will take for the Lakes to cleanse themselves of it. As a result, in some places the fish are healthy and flourishing but the fisheries are closed indefinitely.

The mercury level in fish varies according to their position in the food chain. Those that feed on plankton contain little mercury, but those that eat the plankton eaters contain more, and the fish that eat *them* contain more yet. The farther up the chain that it goes, the more concentrated the mercury becomes. Unhappily, the most desirable fish are the fish-eaters — maskinonge, pike, walleyes, large- and small-mouth bass, and rock bass — and they are the ones that build up the greatest concentrations of the chemical. The mercury level also varies according to the age of the fish, which continues to accumulate the poison during its whole life. Therefore the biggest fish of the best species are those most apt to be saturated with mercury. Government agencies now monitor the situation carefully and direct commercial fishermen to safe areas and safe varieties.

Other contaminants have had great impact. Among them are substances once thought to be great boons to mankind, the chemical pesticides. DDT is the best known; others commonly used are dieldren and chlordane. It is becoming ever more obvious, however, that these chemicals are poisons not only to insects, but to all forms of animal life. In higher animals they affect the reproductive system, the liver, and the growth of body cells; and they have been linked to cancer. When they are used on crops along the lake shores they soon wash into the Lakes, and then the damage begins. As they move up the food chain they become more and more concentrated. If there is a minute amount in the bottom sediment, the worms that live in the sediment will contain fifty times that amount; and the fish that eat the worms will contain five hundred times. As a result, in all of the Lakes except, ironically, Lake Erie, there are fish that contain pesticides in amounts poisonous to man. (It may be that the great array of industry along the Erie shores permits less agriculture than elsewhere, and that for this reason there has been less use of pesticides.) Lake Michigan has the biggest number of fish contaminated by such chemicals. Chub there have been banned as food for several years, and certain lots of other varieties have been removed from sale from time to time because they contained the poisons in amounts detrimental to humans. Coho salmon in that lake have also been found to contain not only DDT but also PCBs (polychlorinated biphenyls, industrial chemicals similar in structure to DDT) above the safe levels for consumption by man. The sale of these fish has also been prohibited.

In 1969 Michigan banned DDT sales, and fruit growers on the Lake Michigan shores have voluntarily given up some of the other more dangerous pesticides. But the chemicals remain in the environment, and no one knows exactly how long the Lakes will need to cleanse themselves. There is strong evidence that the poisons interfere with the reproduction of fish, and we know what they do to some of the animals that eat the fish. In herring gulls the concentration process goes on; their tissues contain fifteen thousand times the amount of DDT that is in the bottom mud. This upsets their calcium metabolism and causes their eggs to break before hatching.

Recently the effect of pesticides on gulls combined dramatically with the effect of the imported alewives (and smelt, another imported fish) during one of their periodic mass deaths. The dead fish washed ashore at the recreational and orchard town of Traverse City, known as one of the prettiest spots in Michigan. Scarcely a gull was to be seen. The natural scavengers no longer existed in that fruit-growing area, so heavily impregnated with pesticides. In 1962 there had been twenty-five hundred gulls' nests on one nearby island; by 1971 there were only three hundred nests on that island. So when the fish-kill washed ashore, the best the residents could do was to rake it into stinking piles.

When commercial fishing was first licensed, the action was more a tax than a control measure and licenses gave rise to more humor than respect. One story tells of an Ontario fisherman who lured

Harbor scene, Port Dover.

his third wife into marriage by the promise of a farm; the deed, when delivered, was a five-dollar fishing license that entitled the bearer to farm all of Lake Huron. But as fishing continued and problems began to arise, each state and province on the Lakes developed some kind of bureau staffed by professional fishery experts. These men gathered periodically and decided what should be done to control their problems. Such groups met as early as 1875. Unfortunately, however, their respective legislatures delegated them no authority; each expert had to return home from the meetings and then recommend to his legislators that the agreed-upon actions be taken. These latter gentlemen, more knowledgeable in political matters of the moment than in fishery problems, would pick and choose among the recommendations, add a few ideas of their own, and pass the results into law. In the end there might be as many as nine different, perhaps even conflicting, laws governing the Great Lakes fisheries.

There seemed to be no general feeling that the fishery situation was urgent; and in the absence of public pressure, members of legislatures do not readily give away authority. It took the movement of the lamprey into the upper Lakes to arouse general alarm. In 1955, a treaty between the United States and Canada established the Great Lakes

Georgian Bay gill net tug. Gill netters are built with large openings well forward through which the nets are raised.

Fishery Commission, which was to control the sea lamprey and carry out research on measures necessary to sustain desirable fish stocks. This was far from being a commission to run the Great Lakes fisheries, but utter destruction of commercial and sports fishing was something voters would not like. Local politicians felt the teeth of the lamprey upon them, and therefore each of the state and provincial fishery units was soon given reasonable authority to respond quickly to problems in concert with the others.

Lamprey control projects were begun first in Lake Superior; the lamprey was not as well established there as in Lakes Huron and Michigan and there was still a chance to save the larger fish. In working out control measures, the fishery men considered the life cycle of the creature. Lampreys move to spawning streams in spring or early summer; the streams and rivers they choose flow with some speed and have gravel bottoms. A spawning pair build a crescent shaped nest on the bottom, deposit their eggs and sperm, cover the nest with sand and gravel, and then die. One female produces sixty thousand eggs. In about two weeks the eggs hatch and tiny, worm-like animals emerge. These creatures live in burrows in the stream bottom for an average of four or five years (although sometimes a lamprey may remain in larval form for as many as twelve years), eating microscopic plants and animals. When the immature lampreys are about eight inches long they emerge from their burrows in late summer, and that autumn or the next spring they move downstream. They live as adults for one or two years, then return to the streams and rivers to spawn and die.

The streams are the obvious places to attack them, for they are rather choosy about the exact spawning places they select. For example, they spawn in only 105 of the more than 2,000 streams flowing into the Canadian side of the Lakes. At first the fishery people developed mechanical and electrical barriers to keep lampreys from passing up the streams. Then they found a chemical that does not harm other fish when used with care, but that does kill the larval form of the lampreys while they are in the stream bottom. Applications of the chemical began in 1958. By 1962, all major Lake Superior streams were being treated. In that year there was a reduction of about 80 percent in the numbers of lampreys coming upstream to spawn. By 1966, the number of spawning lampreys had been reduced to about 10 percent of those that had spawned five years before. The control agencies began to turn their attention to Lakes Huron and Michigan.

Sport fishing for lake trout, Lake Superior.

All of the streams draining into the upper Lakes are checked periodically to see if lamprey are present. When the creatures are discovered, a lamprey control unit goes into action. Such a unit looks something like a combined military company and construction crew. It may have as many as two dozen vehicles, vans, and trailers carrying assorted equipment, and sometimes even a helicopter. For two or three days the men of the unit are busy doing a variety of jobs that range from measuring stream flow to determining just how much of the poison — a chemical with a thirty-four-letter name abbreviated as TFM — is needed. The chemical is then released into the stream and its tributaries at key points in carefully controlled amounts for a period of twelve to eighteen hours. As the treated water passes downstream it is analyzed constantly to make certain that the proper concentration is maintained, for too much of it may kill other fish, and too little will not kill the lamprey. Men of a control unit working in a large river may follow the progress of the TFM for five days before it moves into open water and is dissipated.

Lamprey control has been completed in all of the major lamprey-producing streams in Lakes Superior, Michigan, and Huron; and the streams on the Canadian side of Lake Ontario have been treated. Generally, however, control measures have lagged on the U.S. side for lack of money.

In Lakes Superior and Michigan numbers of hatchery-reared lake trout have been planted, in hopes that they will survive, spawn, and sustain a level of natural reproduction at least as great as that before the lamprey invasion. It will be several years before the results of this work are known. In Lake Huron, by agreement between Michigan and Ontario, a hybrid fish is being planted — a cross between the lake trout and brook trout — called the *splake*. Its synthetic name, which sounds more like a trademark than a fish, may not be enticing; but it grows fast, matures early, and should be able to survive in its Huron environment.

The survival of planted fish can be a problem. Pacific varieties, the chinook salmon and coho salmon, have been planted repeatedly in Lakes Ontario, Erie, Michigan, and Superior. The fish have grown, survived, spawned — and eventually dwindled and disappeared. Only in Lake Michigan has there been some success: planting of cohos in 1966 and 1967 led to tremendous spawning runs in 1967 and 1968. Fishery experts have suggested that the great concentration of alewives in Lake Michigan in those years may have made the difference; at that time and place the coho salmon had a superabundant food supply. Chinook salmon also were planted in Superior and Michigan in 1967 and in Huron in 1968. Several varieties of salmon have been planted on the Canadian shores of Lakes Ontario, Huron, and Superior without notable success. In general, the various kinds of saltwater salmon do not seem able to maintain their populations in the Great Lakes. This is not a complete disadvantage, however. Exotic species may or may not prove desirable in the long run; even the biologists who introduce them cannot be sure. It is better to introduce fish that are subject to natural controls than to bring in species that may take over the fisheries.

Control of the alewife should follow the introduction of new populations of large fish; the coho salmon appears to be a particularly effective predator that can limit the number of the alewives. Additional commercial fishing for alewives might help. The question remains as to what may replace them. They have nearly extinguished the native varieties of small fish; it may be necessary to reintroduce these species or to bring in still others to fill the void as the alewives dwindle. But as the alewives themselves demonstrate, the importation of alien species can be a chancy thing.

Lake Erie, as in most things, is a case unto itself. The tremendous nutrient pollution caused by drainage of human, agricultural, and industrial wastes has

Fishing boats at Grand Bend, Lake Huron.

made it even more productive than be-fore, but of ever less valuable fish. The medium-value yellow perch and white bass are now its best varieties. Smelt, carp, sheepshead, and even goldfish (whose ancestors presumably were re-leased from private pools and aquari-ums) predominate. The sheepshead tend to congregate in the open lake and the carp along the shores; neither variety has much value to either commercial or sport fishermen. There seems to be little chance at present of starting new popu-lations of the better varieties which need cleaner water and more oxygen. Solu-tion of its fishery problems must wait upon the solution of Lake Erie's more basic pollution problems. Lake Ontario differs from Lake Erie in one major way: it now produces few fish of any sort. Otherwise conditions in the two lakes are quite similar. There must be further study of Lake Ontario before any definite conclusions about it are possible.

Various methods are used to catch fish commercially in the Great Lakes. Pound nets, trap nets, and fyke nets are essentially enclosures made of netting; the fish swim in and then cannot find their way out. Seines are nets set parallel to a beach and then drawn ashore, bring-ing with them all of the fish between. Set lines are lines equipped with baited hooks. Trawls are funnel shaped nets drawn through the water by boats. The

fish accumulate in the trawl and are periodically emptied into the boat. Gill nets are nets set vertically in the water. Along their bottom edges are weights that hold them in place and along their top edges are floats that keep them vertical and at the desired level. Fish attempt to swim through the netting and are entangled in it. All of these methods are employed to some degree, but gill-netting is the one in most general use; and it is found on all of the Lakes. Perhaps the next most important is trawling, which has been permitted only in recent years and which is used mainly to catch small fish such as smelt.

Sport fishing is nearer the heart of the average man than is commercial fishing. Whether he sits on a harbor breakwater fishing for carp or goes out in a powerful boat with complicated equipment in search of trout or walleye, the sport fisherman engages in a personal adventure. Even when he comes back empty handed he has gained something. Perhaps the final sizzle of fish in a pan is the least important part of the sport.

Yet sport fishing shares the ups and downs of commercial fishing. Pesticides and mercury pollution affect both. When the lake trout fisheries of Georgian Bay collapsed under lamprey attack in the early 1950s, the extensive charter boat fleet at Meaford and the other Bay

Sport fishing boat trolling beside a typical Lake Superior ore dock.

towns met the same fate as the commercial fleet. No doubt sport fishing has caused some species to become scarce or extinct, just as has commercial fishing. But no one really knows. Tables of figures that show commercial catches over the years are probably not as accurate as the neat columns of print suggest, but they are far better than no records. And the results of sport fishing, by its very nature, have been shown in no records at all.

An intensive study of sport fishing has never been done; now we begin to realize that such a study is needed. Various means of gathering data have been suggested. The most feasible way may be a sampling process by which checks that are made on a limited number of catches indicate the overall picture, though even this approach poses problems. To manage the fisheries, however, we need data on both catches and the value of recreational fishing. Resort areas can arrive at a fairly accurate dollars-and-cents estimate of their yearly income from the influx of fishermen, but how do we measure the value of a weekend fishing expedition to a resident of inner Cleveland or Chicago?

Recreational fishermen may dislike commercial fishermen. They find nets set where they themselves would like to fish; and when sport fishing is poor, commercial fishermen are convenient scapegoats. But a healthy fishery has room for both. Only when both are fishing for the same dwindling species is there real competition, and that is the point at which the control agencies should step in.

The future of the Great Lakes fisheries, both sports and commercial, depends on two things. One is control of pollution. The other is the freedom of professional fishery experts to respond quickly to the changing situation. Being human, they will make occasional mistakes; but being experts in the field, they should make fewer of them than other people. If they are tied down or overridden by politicians we may soon have no fisheries worth the name. If they are allowed to act freely we can look forward to more stable fisheries than in the past, and eventually to more productive fisheries.

Pleasure fishing, Cleveland harbor.

A fast-moving American boat passes cottages flying the Canadian flag. These cottages are on islands along the northeastern shore of Georgian Bay.

6. beaches and boats

It may be a visit to an amusement park on the shores of one of the Lakes or an afternoon at the beach; it may be a vacation at a lakeside cottage or on a boat; it may be a canoe trip through the connecting waters along one of the wilder shores. Great Lakes recreation is made up of many natural delights.

The Lakes first began to draw visitors in the 1800s. One of these travelers was Charles Dickens, who came this way in 1842. He did not think much of what he found on the American side, but became almost hysterical with joy upon crossing the Niagara River into what then was British territory. The Erie Islands, which now adjoin the most polluted waters of all the Lakes, were the resorts of Presidents Harrison and Cleveland during the summer months; and Jay Cooke, the financier, in the 1860s built a summer castle on Gibraltar Island in Lake Erie.

Cooke enjoyed his summer residence until his death in 1905. In 1887, he wrote a description of his residence, which included the account of a typical day. The twenty or twenty-five members of his family and guests followed rather a different schedule than that of any family group we might now find on the Lakes. His description is complete with his personal abbreviations, spelling, and punctuation.

Sailing cruiser and wooded shore.

Marina on Lake Ontario, at Toronto.

We rise at 7. We have prayers with singing & reading the Scriptures at 7:30 & then breakfast. Today our breakfast consisted of Cantelopes, Oatmeal, black-bass, Beefsteak, broiled ham, Apple Sauce, fresh Cucumbers, brown & white bread & butter, Potatoes, hot waffles & maple sugar, Milk, tea & Coffee & peaches & cream. For dinner, Tomato Soup, Boiled bass with egg sauce, Roast Turkey & celery & all the vegetables that are produced in a dozen states north & south of us — & a dessert of fruits & melons puddings & cakes, etc etc. For supper we always have a hearty meal, broiled chickens, hot corn cakes, potatoes, tea, coffee, milk, preserves & cakes etc & frequently about 9:30 or 10 oclock ice cream of domestic manufacture (& delicious) is brought in.

Our amusements are then entered upon, some of the Ladies & girls play croquet, others take their knitting & sit on the rocks under the trees whilst one of their numbers reads from some interesting book. Others sing & play or read in the Library. The boys take to their boats & rowing and the Gentlemen go a fishing & hunting sometimes to the surrounding Islands bringing home supplies of birds, rabbits, quails & always enough fine blackbass to keep the table well supplied. . . . There are swings for the childn & bathing places where the majority of those here enjoy their baths in the open Lake. Boat races, & fishing races for prizes are often inaugurated — & Picnics & excursions to other Islands — some of these lasting two or three days.

A Lake Michigan beach,
north of Muskegon.

More common folk enjoyed bathing at Cedar Point, on the mainland not far from Cooke's island. By the early 1880s steamboats were carrying people to a dock there, and a newspaper in nearby Sandusky, at the behest of the owners of bathhouses on the shore (where bathing suits were rented), was warning people not to bathe along Cedar Point in the nude. A dance hall, restaurants, and more bathhouses followed. There were band concerts and balloon ascensions, and by the turn of the century a resort was well established that has survived to this day as a bathing and amusement park.

While such developments were going on near the centers of population, intrepid vacationists were proceeding farther west along the Lakes. In 1874, John Disturnell published one of his many guide books, this one called *Sailing on the Great Lakes and Rivers of America*. In it he noted of Mackinac, "The bathing in the pure waters of the Strait at this place is truly delightful, affording health and vigor to the human frame," and of Sault Sainte Marie, "Summer visitors annually flock to this place and the Lake Superior country for health and pleasure." In describing Lake Superior he said, "On the North Shore, Canada side, are several fine trout fishing resorts, from fifteen to sixty miles from the Saut [*sic*], where Indians or half-breeds with their canoes have to be employed, often camping out for several days"; and he spoke in glowing terms of Michipicoten Island as a resort.

By the late 1800s, more permanent camps, cottages, and summer hotels had crept along the shores of Georgian Bay and the North Channel, grouped near steamer and rail terminals but scattered much more sparsely through the remoter areas. It remained for the internal combustion engine in car and boat to bring the flood of visitors. Combined with the population explosion, it is the main reason that there are cottages around most of the shores, that wild territory is fast disappearing, and that government park authorities are groping for ways to control the numbers of people that each year flood much of the remaining undeveloped areas.

The unspoiled open spaces and clear waters that attract people bent on recreation have an unfortunate tendency to disappear once the people arrive. Soon the woodland roadsides are lined with advertising signs and hot-dog stands, the snarl of the outboard motor is heard across the bay, and the once-clear water of stream or lake must be strained or chlorinated before we drink it. With recreation, as with all of the other uses of the Lakes, our most pressing need is to learn how we can take advantage of

Amusement park at Cedar Point. The circular look-out car moves up and down the tower in the background.

Yachts cruising the North Channel, Manitoulin Island sometimes come from far beyond the Great Lakes. A cruiser from Florida docks at Little Current.

what nature offers without in the process destroying it.

The sport in which man meets the Lakes most nearly on equal terms is probably that of long-distance racing under sail. Not many of us can participate or would want to, for the boats cost a great deal of money and the crews often take a considerable beating. One yachtsman was quoted as saying, "It is quite easy to simulate the joys of yacht racing in your own home. All you have to do is stand in a very cold shower and tear up twenty-dollar bills." During a recent race from Chicago to Mackinac, only 81 of the 169 boats that started actually reached Mackinac three days later. The remainder, faced with 70-mph winds and pounded by 15-foot waves, took refuge along the Michigan shore. The log of one of the winning yachts, the 34-foot sloop *Kalte Ente,* describes how a crew member, off watch, was asleep on the cabin floor when the bilge pump failed. Exhausted, he did not feel the water rising around him until the motion of the boat threw a foil-wrapped meat loaf against his face and woke him up.

This sort of thing is not what most people would call recreation; but leisurely cruising in boats, both power and sail, provides one of the best ways to see the Lakes as they really are. The growth of marinas to provide service to cruising yachts at most large cities and the number of yachts from those cities that one finds in such relatively isolated waters as the North Channel are indications that a great many people feel the same way. Lake Michigan, for example, the same body of water that scattered over half the boats in that Mackinac race, has marinas and yacht clubs that welcome visiting cruisers at Chicago, Waukegan, Milwaukee, Charlevoix, and other ports including Frankfort, which sheltered some fifty of those battered racers. The biggest concentration of yacht harbors on any of the Lakes is at Saint Clair Shores, on the American side of Lake Saint Clair, where over five thousand boats are berthed in a space of a mile. On the more sparsely inhabited shores of the Lakes formal harbor facilities are not common; but the wilder, more natural surroundings are the attractions.

Sometimes these natural surroundings have their drawbacks as well. Two cruising boats were tied up side by side in one small harbor. A yachtsman, stirring at 2:00 A.M., looked over, saw a light in the cabin of the other boat, and called across to ask what was happening. "What else would we be doing at 2:00 in the morning," came the answer, "but swatting mosquitoes?"

Even though the cost and complications of a cruising boat limit the number of people who can enjoy one, smaller

*In the harbor at Midland, Ontario, pleasure boats and
swimming youngsters share the water with lake freighters.*

Skier and water patterns.

boats have become almost as common as autos. At times, unhappily, this has led a few automobilists who never have really learned to drive their cars, to convert their bad driving habits into truly horrible boating habits: running powerful boats at high speed through bathers and anchorages without regard to the danger or discomfort caused others, ignoring the rights of sailboats, and even on occasion upsetting smaller craft. If such people are not soon grounded by legal difficulties, however, there is always the glorious probability that they will run full speed into a rock. Then more judicious boatmen will inherit the waters, for there are few better ways to savor the enjoyment of the Lakes than to putter around on them in a boat. From the boy or girl in a canoe to the yachtsman or woman aboard a grand seventy-footer, the people who are afloat best understand the moods of the Lakes.

The next best way to enjoy the changing natural beauties of the Great Lakes chain is to live on one of its shores. This also is the most popular way and people without number do it. The kinds of shelters that can be found are infinitely variable, from such beautiful waterside homes as those at Vermilion, on Lake Erie or those along the Saint Clair River — homes in both places that are more nearly year-around residences than summer cottages — to a tent camp at one of the wilder spots on Lake Superior. Between these extremes there is a vast range of what can be rented, leased, bought, or built. There also is a considerable choice of location: sandy or rocky shore, shallow or deep water, on an island or near a highway. But gradually, inexorably, the cottages and cabins are creeping around all of the shores; and one day the only uninhabited areas will be the government parks. Ironically, man's very pursuit of natural beauty diminishes what he seeks.

Owning a summer home or cottage on the lakeshore has one disadvantage: it ties you to a particular place. One of the enjoyments of the Great Lakes region is sightseeing, and in order to see sights you must travel. There are many things to see if you do.

Fast boat and spray.

The tremendous growth of pleasure boating has spurred the development of marinas and boat harbors along the shores of the Lakes. Here is a marina at Cedar Point, Lake Erie.

Boat harbor at Grand Bend, Lake Huron.

Modern cottage on one of the islands in Georgian Bay.

Sailboat race at Toronto harbor on Lake Ontario.

Cruisers find pleasant harbors, such as this one at the fishing port of Bayfield, on Lake Huron.

Pleasure boats on the Detroit River.

Cottage in the dunes.

From the tulips of Holland, Michigan, to the canoe country of Quetico, at the head of Lake Superior, there is a wide selection of natural beauties to enjoy. There are also historical items beyond count, including the reconstructed mission fort of Sainte Marie, the first white establishment on the Great Lakes, which was destroyed by its French builders in 1649 to keep it from falling into the hands of invading Iroquois Indians; or the equally careful reconstruction of Commodore Perry's flagship, the brig *Niagara,* in which he won the battle of Lake Erie in 1813. The former is near Midland, Ontario; the latter is at Erie, Pennsylvania. There are a number of good marine museums, among them one maintained at Vermilion by the Great Lakes Historical Society, one maintained at Detroit by that city, and one maintained at Wasaga Beach by the Province of Ontario.

Visitors may take in-plant tours through industrial operations ranging from steel mills to ketchup factories (usually children below a given age are not permitted on these tours for obvious reasons; one slip and Susie could come to an early end as a steel rail or Willie as tomato paste). And many things that are not designed to educate or amaze can still be quite surprising to strangers. For example, a lot of people do not know that along the western coast of Michigan

At Erie, Pennsylvania, the masts, rigging, and sails of the reconstructed U.S. Brig Niagara, *Commodore Perry's flagship at the Battle of Lake Erie, rise against the sky.*

rail cars are put on steamers to carry them across the lake, or that conversely, at Severn Falls near Georgian Bay yachts are put on a railroad that carries them up or down the drop in the Severn River. Shipwatchers can enjoy the passing marine traffic along the Saint Lawrence River, at the Welland Canal, in the Saint Clair River, or at the place that seems to attract them most of all, the locks at Sault Sainte Marie. And there is wildlife to observe for those who are interested, and scenery to be seen. The list of possibilities is endless.

Pontoon houseboats, such as this one, can be used on quiet days on the Lakes themselves and on every day on many tributary rivers. Port Franks, Ontario, near Lake Huron.

The most northern lock of the Trent Waterways, at Port Severn. The lockmaster (upper right) opens the gates that let the cruising craft out at the level of Georgian Bay.

Canoe in voyageur country.

Wherever people go, however, their very numbers cause stresses and strains. The problems of keeping them from spoiling the places they enjoy are clearly illustrated in the canoe country west of Lake Superior along the Minnesota-Ontario boundary. This is the route the voyageurs followed as they headed west and north from the Great Lakes. On the American side there is the Boundary Waters Canoe Area, on the Canadian side the Quetico Provincial Park. Together they make up a region that attracts more visitors than any other wilderness area in North America, and the visitors increase at a rate of about 8 percent annually. If that rate continues until the year 2000, the region will have over two million visitor-days of use each year, which almost certainly will ruin it. Visitor management, the term used by the U.S. Forest Service, will therefore have to include more and more restrictions such as limiting the size of camping parties and the time that parties can spend at any one place, requiring visitors to make advance reservations, and sending parties over specified routes.

Another struggle is to keep the quality of the water at a high level. Without pure water the region would lose much of its value. To stem the growth of pollution the U.S. authorities are trying to develop latrines that will not leach wastes, yet that will meet "wilderness

Marina at Milwaukee, Lake Michigan.

Marina at Marquette, Lake Superior, in the shadow of a giant ore dock.

A heavily built cruiser, shown at Little Current, North Channel on Manitoulin Island.

concepts"; and they are banning the use of detergents and disposable food and drink containers that cannot be burned. With all of these internal problems, the area also faces attacks from outside: there are political pressures by groups on both sides of the border that want to exploit the mining and lumber resources there.

Recreational areas that are closer to the centers of population and that have been in use for a period of years face other problems. One of these is Wasaga Beach on Georgian Bay, about a hundred miles north of Toronto. On a summer weekend it will draw fifty thousand visitors. Over the past half century it has grown from a nine-mile stretch of open sand on which there were a few hotels and cottages to a sort of unorganized amusement park on the water, with bingo games, rides, and similar diversions in addition to the bathing. From the earliest days of settlement the long beach served as a highway; and cars still pick their way around groups of bathers, bicyclists, and children chasing rubber balls. Crowds have brought with them the problems of trash and pollution. For the past few years the Province of Ontario has been trying to bring some order out of the chaos. It has made the beach proper into a provincial park and is banning cars from it, it has drawn up an $18 million development plan that is projected into the 1980s, and it is trying to wrest the remaining unused land in the area from the hands of commercial developers. But it has a long way to go. The owners of various entertainments who have resisted even the setting of limits on the volume of the loudspeakers outside their places of business will scarcely define "protection and development" of the area — the stated aims of the provincial plan — in the same terms as those who still come there to observe rare shore birds along the water's edge.

Worse yet are the difficulties at many of the beaches that are truly close to large cities. The problems along the Lake Erie shores near Cleveland and at the mouth of the Detroit River are notorious. Often the only thing the authorities can do is to close the beaches. Pollution at these areas, however, is not directly the fault of the people who would use them for recreation, but rather that of the municipalities and industries that defile the waters. Corrective action here must be part of a much wider program.

A fast boat runs parallel to a beach on Lake Huron, near Grand Bend.

On Manitoulin Island, at Little Current on the North Channel. Pleasure boats tie up across a park from the town's main street.

Beach scene, Georgian Bay.

Small sailboat.

Pollution by noise has also begun to afflict resort areas, although it has not yet drawn much official attention. We worry about the noises caused at urban airports, but so far there has been no concerted effort to lessen the sounds that can blight recreational spots. The danger signal comes when people begin to talk of moving to a quieter place. That may work now, but if the volume continues to swell will there be a quieter place to retreat to in the year 2000? We may find it quieter just to stay home.

Of course, some judgment is necessary in condemning noise. In an amusement park it is to be expected, and a ferris wheel or merry-go-round without the garish music would be tame indeed, or a bingo game without the barker's patter would attract few players. But the vast numbers of lakeside resorts draw people because of the natural attractions, and any noise louder than the breaking of waves destroys those attractions. The internal-combustion engine that pollutes our city air is the main villain here as well, but in a different way: cars, unless they are in bad repair or driven by adolescents in need of proving their manhood, are usually quiet enough; but unmuffled motorcycles, dune buggies, minibikes, and outboard motors produce sounds to shatter the nerves of all but their operators. Occasionally some child may get a supply of firecrackers to

*Sailing is especially popular.
A boat leaves harbor, taking a
willing crew for an afternoon
sail.*

Sail and power. North Channel, Manitoulin Island.

Canoe at sunset.

thicken the din. Luckily there seems to be a growing reaction, for canoes and bicycles are regaining popularity. It seems likely, however, that legal sanctions much like those against other forms of pollution will be needed to control the worst of the noise polluters.

There are two kinds of recreational pleasures — those found among groups of people and those found in solitude. One can have pleasure in a crowded nightclub or alone in a canoe on a quiet stream. Traditionally we have thought of the Great Lakes region, with the exception of a few cities, as an area where we could get away from the crowds. Some of the shores are still like that, but they are shrinking. Where ten years ago there was one cottage, today there are five; where ten years ago there was one boat, today there are ten. By the year 2000, it is probable that the only wild terrain left in the region will be in government parks, and even that may be a sort of ersatz wilderness with public toilets.

Thus by the end of the century we may have to look elsewhere for solitude, if indeed any solitude is left anywhere. The growth of populations, the desire of small towns to become bigger, the urge of regional planners to put something — anything — in those blank areas on the map — all these will bring more people to what have been the remote, quiet spots. Barring plagues and nuclear wars, it seems inevitable. With work and good planning we may be able to keep the Lakes fairly clean and decent, but we can't keep away the people.

We may enjoy our favorite solitudes as long as they last, but one day we either will find a factory in the middle of them or discover that they have become housing developments. Either way they will cease being quiet places insulated from humanity. There still will be pleasant spots on the Lakes, but they no longer will be remote. They will be like the outdoors areas of the older, more crowded nations, areas which are carefully maintained and are even beautiful, but which are seldom wild. Instead of canoeing alone, we will canoe in flotillas. And instead of people who enjoy the pleasures of solitude, the Lakes will draw those who prefer having fun in company.

Small sailboats provide good fun.

*Sewage caked on the bank of Ohio's Ottawa River
near its mouth at the western end of Lake Erie.*

7. pollution

Ripe and recognizable sewage flushes down the Detroit River into Lake Erie, with the result that the gray-green waves of the lake wash up dead fish and algae on its western beaches. The once prosperous commercial fisheries of Lake Saint Clair are closed because of mercury poisoning. On Lake Ontario oil soaked dead ducks float in the harbor eddies. Pesticides from surrounding orchards have saturated Lake Michigan fish and hindered their reproduction. Massive new power plants on the shores of Lake Huron may raise its temperature and change its character. Mining operations near Lake Superior throw their waste into its water. The Great Lakes have become the dumping ground of the megalopolis fast growing around them.

The population explosion, the technological explosion, and a clock that seems to run ever faster are our most acute problems. Great cities standing elbow to elbow cannot act in the same way as small ones with miles between, but our habits of living were formed yesterday when there were not enough of us to overwhelm the Lakes with our debris. Today we are doing just that. Technology outruns our best intentions. Useful factories are built that drain small and supposedly harmless amounts of waste into nearby waters; then we discover too late that mercury in the waste has made our fish unfit to eat. Because of the enormous damage caused by phosphates in our detergents, we rush into use new detergents that contain other chemicals; but we have no time to examine these chemicals first and learn what they in turn may do to us.

One further complicating factor has been an economic explosion

that causes us to throw things away at a steadily increasing rate. Beer cans, paper diapers, and contraceptives discarded on the shores of the Great Lakes often find their way into the Lakes. Joseph Wood Krutch has equated gross national product with the gross national garbage pile. Others point out that the refuse produced in the United States has increased at the rate of 4 percent per year, almost exactly the same as the GNP.

While we struggle to make sense out of our interlocking problems that comprise pollution we are beset on the one hand by that minority of city fathers and industrialists who insist that they have a God-given right to dump anything they please into the public water and air, and on the other by those romantics who seem to think that to cleanse the planet all mankind should drop dead immediately. The real answer lies somewhere between. We must use the Great Lakes for our purposes, but we must not destroy them; for we then destroy ourselves.

When pollution is mentioned, our first thought usually is of sewage. Disposal of the excrement produced by communities of people has been recognized as a problem for some time. Around the Great Lakes the initial answer was usually to pipe it directly into the water. As

Smoke and fumes are given out by a factory on the Welland Canal between Lakes Ontario and Erie.

long as communities were small and far apart that was a workable solution. The sewage was dissipated throughout the lake, the microorganisms in the water attacked it and broke it down into inorganic chemicals, and the chemicals fertilized algae and other plant life which produced oxygen and fed the smaller aquatic animals. It was all part of the natural cycle of life, the same process that goes on in one form or another on land or in the water.

As populations grew, people began to sniff the water and realize that something more should be done to the sewage before it was discharged. The first step was to pass it through screens and shredders into a series of settling tanks; after half an hour to an hour and a half in the tanks, it was released into the streams and lakes. This process is known today as primary treatment, and in many places it is still the only treatment. Secondary treatment, which our more advanced communities have added, removes more solids and converts the remaining organic matter to inorganic chemicals. In addition, it chlorinates the outflow to kill any disease germs present before the stuff is released. The result of secondary treatment is a fluid that neither carries disease nor stinks like raw sewage. Although a good deal of untreated or partially treated sewage is still dumped into the Lakes, many cities

Beach near the western end of Lake Erie. The green algae and dead fish show the polluted condition of the water.

now release antiseptic sewage, much of it converted to inorganic form.

Until recently we thought that at this point our problems were ended. Instead, they have just begun. The inorganic chemicals are themselves at least as good fertilizers as the original sewage, and our booming populations are pouring so much of this fertilizer into the Lakes that the algae and other forms of aquatic plant life that thrive upon it are growing at tremendously accelerated rates. They not only cloud and clog the water, but when in due course they die they are about as unpleasant as sewage itself. Their decomposition also draws oxygen from the water, thus killing or limiting the animal life in it. One pound of phosphorus can produce a thousand pounds of algae, so that the amount of decomposing organic matter that the lake must handle far exceeds the quantity of the sewage put into it.

And we have still further difficulties. Adding to the water an amount of fertilizer at least equal to that provided by sewage are a host of industrial processes ranging from canning to wood pulping (these may or may not pass their wastes through some sort of treatment before releasing them). The difficulties are also augmented by agricultural processes, chief among which are the concentration of animals in feed pens, with subsequent flushing of manure into the water systems, and the replacement of manure as fertilizer on the fields by chemicals that also wash eventually into the Lakes. But probably a greater problem than any of these is the flow of detergents which are not easily filtered out and which move through our disposal plants in great

Paper mills, such as this one at Thunder Bay, Lake Superior, must install complex and expensive equipment to avoid polluting the water.

quantities. The detergents that were first introduced were so sudsy that they would never stop foaming. When used by one housewife they passed through sewage disposal plants and water purification plants and emerged still foaming from the kitchen tap of some other housewife. To end this disquieting trait, manufacturers produced detergents with a new sudsing agent that broke down readily after use. But they kept the phosphate base for detergents because it softens the wash water and reinforces the sudsing agent effectively. Unhappily, phosphates also are excellent fertilizers.

The impact of all this is best seen at the western end of Lake Erie. It is the most shallow of the Great Lakes and its western end is particularly shallow. Into this basin pours the sewage and factory waste, treated and otherwise, from the vast Detroit-Windsor metropolitan area. There is not enough water in the shallow lake to dissipate it. As a result, algal growth has been tremendous, dead algae are rotting on the beaches, and organic material that is falling to the bottom and decomposing there has used up the oxygen. One result is that mayflies, which a few years ago swarmed along the western shores of the lake in great numbers during spring and early summer, and which provided both fish food and fish bait, have disappeared. In their larval form

*Trash dump on the shore
of Lake Erie. Ashtabula County, Ohio.*

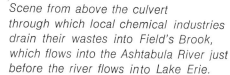

Scene from above the culvert through which local chemical industries drain their wastes into Field's Brook, which flows into the Ashtabula River just before the river flows into Lake Erie.

Water pollution.

they lived on the bottom of the lake, but now there is no oxygen there for them. The western end of Lake Erie is the most polluted spot on all of the Great Lakes, but others are not far behind.

What can we do about it? Processes have been developed for removing phosphates from sewage, but they require additional equipment and extra cost. Depending on the size of the city, the cost of removing phosphates varies from three to six dollars per person per year — the larger the city, the smaller the cost per capita. The total cost for a given city may appear to be overwhelming, but if we consider that the cost to each individual would be no more than one tankful of gasoline or one carton of cigarettes per year, the price of keeping the Lakes clean seems quite modest.

A number of cities have banned the sale of detergents with phosphate bases. The other fertilizing chemicals, however, plus all the sewage still in organic form, continue to pour into the Lakes. Milwaukee, Wisconsin, for a number of years has used its sewage to make fertilizer which is sold commercially. This has the double value of returning the sewage to the land and keeping it out of Lake Michigan. A much more costly but also much more extensive method is

Water pollution.

being tried at Muskegon, Michigan, under the auspices of the U.S. Federal Water Quality Administration. Sewage from twelve communities is piped inland, away from Lake Michigan and the smaller lakes that have received it in the past. Fifteen miles away in an almost uninhabited area of sand dunes it is processed, sterilized, and stored in large lagoons, then piped to irrigation rigs that spray the liquid fertilizer over about six thousand acres of formerly unproductive soil.

The Muskegon plan was not approved without difficulty. The history of its development illustrates some of the human problems that also must be considered as we move toward solutions. Working together, Roderick Dittmer, director of planning for Muskegon County, and John R. Sheaffer, of the University of Chicago's Center for Urban Studies, decided that the idea resolved not only the immediate problems of sewage disposal, but also some other problems of Muskegon County. The county did not have the agriculture needed to balance its industrial capacity and it was unable to use its several inland lakes for recreation because they had become so polluted. The plan would solve these difficulties.

Matted algae in the water and on the shore is found in Lakes Erie and Ontario. This scene (center photo) and the closeup (right) is on the northern shore of Lake Erie, east of Port Dover.

It would also solve the sewage disposal problem, at least until the year 2000.

At that point, however, the Michigan State Water Resources Commission vetoed the idea — there was no need to plan that far ahead and it was much too expensive a project anyway. But even though the state agency disapproved the suggestion, the fifteen-man board of Muskegon County Commissioners, without regard to party politics, supported the idea. They retained consulting engineer William J. Bauer of Chicago to do the actual design and were able to get the U.S. Department of Housing and Urban Development to pay some of the fees. After the design was completed, however, the plan faced more trouble. The cities of Muskegon and Muskegon Heights had their own plans for much cheaper systems that would continue to pour treated sewage into the water. Advocates of these systems considered the Bauer plan far too complex and futuristic.

In the midst of the local political struggle that followed, the S. D. Warren Paper Company, a division of Scott Paper and one of the three major industries of Muskegon, asked Messrs.

Debris and death, washed up on a Great Lakes beach.

Dittmer, Sheaffer, and Bauer for detailed information about their scheme. N. J. Lardieri, Warren's director of pollution control, quickly saw that the proposal would solve the pollution problem at one stroke and for an extended time (discharge from the paper mill would make up as much as 55 percent of the wastes going into the system) and that its costs could be amortized in a business-like manner. Warren put its weight behind the idea and other local industries then began to follow.

Michigan Congressman Guy Vander Jagt then became interested. As ranking Republican member of the Conservation and Natural Resources Subcommittee of the House Government Operations Committee, he was in a good position to interest federal agencies, foremost among them the Federal Water Quality Administration. He also discussed the Muskegon plan with members of the presidential staff. As one result, Sheaffer received a letter from President Nixon expressing interest. David Dominick, head of FWQA, wrote a highly favorable letter to the congressman, who thereupon carried it personally to the governor of Michigan, William Milliken. The governor soon took a tour of the state, with a stop at Muskegon; and not long after his return to the state capitol the Michigan Water Resources Commission announced that the Muskegon plan was a

Even where clear water breaks on the beach, one can find trash piles. Georgian Bay.

*Steel mills, such as this
one on the Cuyahoga River in Cleveland,
discharge their wastes into the river.*

good one after all. This announcement was followed in due course by an agreement that the federal government would pay 55 percent of the construction costs, the state 25 percent, and Muskegon County the remainder.

The barren area selected for farming is well suited for irrigation and fertilization of the sort it will receive. The sand and gravel of the soil, plus a network of drainage wells, will carry off the excess water which eventually will return in purified form to the rivers and lakes. The crop best suited for such an area is corn, and the value of the corn that could be grown is estimated at $740,000 per year. This idea originated at Pennsylvania State University, where a smaller experimental setup of the same kind gave spectacular results, among them harvests that were increased threefold. It is only a little more subtle form — though a vastly more expensive one — of the use of human fertilizer that has been practiced by peasant farmers in many parts of the world for centuries, and it comes closer to the natural cycle of life processes than any other disposal system acceptable to urban man. For that reason it may well prove to be the most workable.

The U.S. Corps of Engineers has prepared feasibility studies for application of this same idea to two of the biggest problem areas on the Great Lakes, those of Detroit and Cleveland, as well as to the highly urbanized Chicago area. Technically there seems to be no reason that similar systems could not be set up for those cities. But the studies do not consider what probably are the biggest obstacles, the complex political difficulties involved. Each of these metropolitan areas is many times the size of Muskegon, and the political problems encountered in each would no doubt be increased at least proportionately over those of Muskegon.

Use of sewage as fertilizer, plus techniques to keep chemical fertilizer from washing quickly into nearby waters, may control much of the nutrient pollution now caused by agriculture. But agriculture is also the source of insecticide pollution. Insecticides used on farmlands and orchards find their way into the water just as do the fertilizers. They are extremely stable chemicals that do not break down readily by natural processes. Since World War II, DDT especially has been used in tremendous quantities. Traces of it have been discovered in organisms in all parts of the world, from the far Arctic to the far Antarctic. And as we know, some of the fish in Lake Michigan are found to contain in their flesh sufficiently high levels of this and other insecticides to render sterile both themselves and the gulls that feed on

Colorful buoys used in checking water conditions. At the Canada Centre for Inland Waters.

them, and probably to poison human beings who might eat them.

Agriculture makes another dubious contribution to the Lakes and the areas that adjoin them. Mercury salts are used to spray seedcrops in order to retard damage from fungi. These salts not only find their way into the water and add their bit to a serious variety of chemical pollution, but they are absorbed into the flesh of game birds such as ducks and pheasants that feed along the shores, making the flesh poisonous for human consumption. The tissues of ducks taken from the Lake Saint Clair area have contained more than twice the acceptable amount of mercury.

The answer to pollution caused by pesticides and fungicides at first seems obvious: simply prohibit those substances that cause the most damage. But stringent prohibition often must wait upon the development of less harmful substitutes for the dangerous materials. Although DDT has now been banned by the U.S. government, bans on similar chemicals may not follow until the government can offer farmers and fruit growers a reasonable substitute. Otherwise it could bring economic calamity upon a whole area.

The dumping into the Great Lakes and their tributaries of all sorts of industrial wastes began just as did the dumping of sewage. The industries were small and far apart, the amounts of waste they produced were comparatively little, and the waters were extensive enough to absorb and dissipate them. Then the cities and the industries gradually became larger, and gradually we have reached the situation that exists today. If we can solve the problem of sewage disposal we no doubt will solve at the same time the problem of disposing of factory wastes that unduly fertilize the waters. There remains the problem of the wastes that simply poison them.

Perhaps the industrial pollutant that has the most obvious results is oil. The Cuyahoga River, which drains into Lake Erie at Cleveland, recently caught fire, damaging two bridges. It was, of course, the waste oil floating on it that actually burned. Oil of this sort fouls our beaches, irreparably gums the feathers of water birds that it touches, and above all kills fish and shellfish. Oil comes not only from factories; waste oil from the filling stations of one medium-size city alone can add up to twenty thousand gallons per month. Some ocean-going ships have a habit of pumping waste oil overboard — a bad enough habit at sea, but in the restricted waters of the Lakes it is disastrous. Both U.S. and Canadian authorities do their best to police oil pumping by ships. In Canada the Department of Transport uses airplanes

The Grand River of Ontario looks delightful on a sunny day, but it is the most polluted Canadian river that runs into Lake Erie.

Marshes along the southern shore of Lake Erie, the most polluted Great Lake, still shelter much wildlife, such as this American Egret seen at Crane Creek State Park, Ohio.

to spot vessels that are pumping oil and to take photos that are used as evidence against them.

In 1969, the U.S. Federal Water Pollution Control Administration coordinated a joint operation by the state of Michigan and federal authorities to remove many thousands of gallons of bunker and lubricating oil from the wreck of the German ship *Nordmeer,* which had run aground three years previously off the city of Alpena, Michigan, in Lake Huron. The wreck had broken in two and was threatening to break up completely. This would release some forty-seven thousand gallons of oil into Lake Huron. The actual pumping out of the wreck was done by a commercial firm managed by Robert Massey, a former frogman and experienced diver. Working in calm periods through the stormy month of November, Bob Massey and his salvage crew pumped the oil out of the wreck a little at a time, into tanks in the salvage tug. Thus an oil spill was averted that could have caused a slick of a thousand square miles on the surface of Lake Huron.

Oil causes obvious damage, although its toxic effects on fish have not been fully appreciated until recently. The results of dumping other industrial wastes into our waters are less evident. The cyanide released by steel mills on the Cuyahoga River kills fish in the river, but what does it do when it reaches Lake Erie? Other industries dispose of arsenic, lead, and cadmium by throwing them into the water. No one really knows all the substances that industry dumps into the Lakes, and no one really knows what they may do to us.

It also is possible for air pollution to cause water pollution. At Sudbury, Ontario, thirty-odd miles north of Georgian Bay, copper and nickel smelters pour fumes into the atmosphere. Sulfur

Off-shore platform, in Canadian waters of Lake Erie. The underwater wells that have been drilled so far have been mainly for natural gas, but there appears to be oil under the lake as well and pressure will grow to drill for it. Such drilling carries a constant threat of accidental spills that would damage the environment.

dioxide coming from the stacks is converted to other forms of sulfur, particularly sulfuric acid, as it reaches the air. Much of the nearby vegetation is killed by smelter pollution, and some forms such as white pine which are especially sensitive have been damaged as far as eighty miles away. Many water plants have disappeared from the small lakes near the smelters, but scientists inves-

At Sudbury, Ontario, north of Georgian Bay, nickel and copper smelters pollute the air with materials that turn into sulphuric acid and kill the surrounding vegetation and wildlife. Sulphuric acid in rain and snow has seriously polluted small lakes along the shore of Georgian Bay. The central chimney in this picture, said to be the tallest in the world, is intended to shoot the pollutants so high that they will decay before coming down.

tigating pollution in the area found one positive feature — it also eliminated mosquitoes and black flies.

On the northern shore of Georgian Bay lie the La Cloche Mountains, first named by the voyageurs and now in part enclosed by Killarney Provincial Park. This area inspired an entire school of Canadian painters known as the Group of Seven; and one of the larger lakes there, just inland from Georgian Bay, is named O.S.A. Lake, for the Ontario Society of Artists. Today O.S.A. Lake has been called one of the most seriously polluted lakes in Canada. The waters are so acid that they are deadly to most kinds of fish, and an analysis of rain and snow indicates that there is a steady fall of sulfuric acid in the region. Other La Cloche lakes are in similar condition. Ironically, these lakes originally were among the purest in North America because the quartzite rocks on which they lie are so insoluble; but for the same reason there are no alkalis in the water that might neutralize the acid.

Industry attempts to disperse noxious fumes by building high stacks, but in this case it appears that the method simply carried the poisons into a particularly vulnerable area. It seems probable that the emissions were also carried to Georgian Bay itself, but that body of water is sufficiently large that no obvious damage has been done to it.

Now the International Nickel Company has built at Sudbury a new stack, called the tallest in the world. The theory is that this stack will shoot the sulfur dioxide so high that it will not come down until it has decayed into some other form. The actual results remain to be seen.

The prime example of unwitting chemical pollution is the pollution by mercury. Few people thought that inorganic mercury was an especially dangerous substance. If it was dumped into the waters of the Lakes in moderate quantities, what harm could result? Probably it would sink straight to the bottom; at worst it might kill a few fish. Paper mills used mercury compounds to prevent slime from forming during their manufacturing; chemical works used mercury to separate chlorine from brine solutions. Mercury was not even listed as one of the chemicals to be tested for by that pollution watchdog, the U.S. Federal Water Quality Administration. Then in the spring of 1970, the Ontario government found mercury in the tissues of fish caught in Lake Saint Clair. The Great Lakes had a new pollution crisis.

Over the past twenty years there have been outbreaks of mercury poisoning in Japan with nearly fifty deaths and many cases of illness as a result. There it was discovered that mercury discharged into

the ocean by various factories had been absorbed by fish which in turn had formed a main part of the diet of the people. In Sweden, the deaths of large numbers of birds was traced to mercury fungicides used on crops. In both of these cases the harm to people and to birds was done by the highly toxic form, methyl mercury. And that was the form that now was being found in Great Lakes fish. But it was mainly inorganic mercury that had been dumped into the Lakes. What could be happening?

Investigators found that in water, bacteria changed inorganic mercury into methyl mercury, which then was absorbed by lower forms of life that were in turn eaten by the fish. Mercury did no damage to the fish, which continued a healthy and presumably happy existence; but it remained in their flesh until they were caught by sport or commercial fishermen. Then if it was present in sufficient amounts it would poison anyone who ate the catch. The early symptoms of mercury poisoning are such vague things as headaches and irritability, symptoms common to a great many people in our high pressure society. Thus it is quite possible that there have been any number of mild cases of mercury poisoning that never have been diagnosed.

The mercury in Lake Saint Clair was traced to a chlor-alkali plant at Sarnia,

Toledo recently expanded its sewage disposal plant. This aeration tank (left), shown under construction, demonstrates how such tanks work. Pumps in the building will force air through the pipes to the grid at bottom, where it will be released. At right, a general view of the aeration tanks.

Ontario; mercury farther downstream in the Detroit River was traced to a similar plant at Wyandotte, Michigan. These factories had been in operation for some twenty years, and without doubt had poured sizable amounts of mercury into the water during most of that time. The various goverments involved on both sides of the border made extensive tests of the mercury in fish caught in these waters and in Lake Erie, into which they flow. In Lake Saint Clair, fish averaged five times the amount of mercury acceptable to man. Mercury pollution continued at a high level in the western end at Lake Erie, that most sinned-against part of the Great Lakes, but gradually lessened as the fishermen moved farther east. Once east of Point Pelee on the Canadian side and Sandusky on the American side of the lake, it still was safe to catch fish for the commercial market. But the thriving commercial fisheries of Lake Saint Clair were closed entirely, and commercial fishing in western Lake Erie was banned. Later, during the summer of 1970, the Canadian authorities also prohibited commercial fishing at the eastern end of Lake Ontario and in the upper Saint Lawrence River into which it drains. This ban was the result of mercury originating at a plant a considerable distance inland in New York State.

Drain entering Field's Brook. Once a country stream, the brook now drains wastes from local chemical industries. This brook enters the Ashtabula River just before the river feeds into Lake Erie. (See also top left photo, page 152.)

Stringent action by government agencies has turned off most of the mercury that was flowing into the Lakes. But we are left with a great store of inorganic mercury on the bottom, and we know that it is slowly and steadily being converted to methyl mercury. No one really can say how long it will remain with us; estimates on the time required for natural forces to cleanse the water of it range from ten to one hundred years. Various solutions have been suggested: dredging out those mercury deposits that have been identified on the bottom, releasing some other chemical that will combine with mercury and render it inert, or trying to clean the bottom with detergents. All seem likely to cause as much damage as they cure, and none are simple or inexpensive. As yet there seems to be no really good answer.

Mercury until now has given us our best example of what the dumping of apparently innocent substances into the water can do to us. But who knows what surprises tomorrow may bring?

Industry may cause pollution in still another way. On Lake Superior — thus far the least polluted of our Great Lakes — one plant that concentrates iron ore into taconite pellets discharges waste materials directly into the lake. Two-thirds of the low-grade ore brought into the plant consists of valueless material. Thus for every ton of taconite that it produces, it flushes two tons of unwanted waste into the lake — an average load of sixty thousand tons per day. Every twelve days this plant dumps as much sediment into the water as do all the streams and rivers along the U.S. shore of the whole lake in a full year. This has been going on for thirteen years. Some of the waste contains chemicals that may speed up the aging process of the lake, but probably more important is the simple effect of all that dirt thrown regularly into the water. The lake has become cloudy for some eighteen miles around; particles of the dust are held in suspension throughout the area and gradually are being carried even farther away; fish and other organisms are killed.

Other taconite plants around Lake Superior release their wastes into closed pools that prevent major contamination of the water. But that method costs more money. And the particular company involved seems determined not to accept the expenses that are normal for its competitors. When, after much maneuvering by the company, the state of Minnesota still brought pressure to clean up the mess, the company filed a suit against the state, claiming that its water quality standards were too high!

Without the presence of human beings, the Great Lakes would eventually cleanse themselves of most pollutants that enter them. It would take a long time, however; and today we are pouring assorted guck into them at a rate much faster than nature can handle. Not only have we overwhelmed the natural biological processes for breaking down sewage, but we far outdo the natural drainage from lake to lake and finally down the Saint Lawrence. It takes 190 years for Lake Superior to empty and re-fill itself and 100 years for Lake Michigan to do so. Twenty years are needed for Lake Huron to complete the process, 8 years for Lake Ontario, and 3 years for Lake Erie.

All lakes age. The water flowing out tends to erode the channels, permit still more water to flow out, and lower the water level. The inflow of water tends to carry sediment which is deposited on the bottom of the lake, gradually filling it up and making it shallower. As more materials are brought into the lake by streams, rivers, and even the wind, nutrients are naturally among them. Algae and other organisms thrive on the nutrients, organic matter falls to the bottom and decomposes, and much of the oxygen near the bottom is used up. The lake fills up with decaying matter as well as with the sediment washed into it. As it becomes shallower it becomes warmer; cold-water fish disappear and those preferring warm water thrive. Growing shallower yet, the lake finally reaches a point where it receives enough light from its surface that plants can take root on the bottom. Then later it becomes a habitat for plants that root on the bottom but float on the surface — water lilies, for example — and finally plants develop that root on the bottom and rise firmly into the air. Shortly after this, the lake is no longer a lake; it is a swamp.

The Great Lakes, geologically speaking, are quite new, so this process should be rather limited. Also, they are so much larger than the usual lake that it should take millions of years for them to age — such a long time in fact that the whole process could be interrupted by some other development such as a new southward thrusting of glaciers. But since human beings have arrived on their shores, the Lakes have begun to age more quickly. This is particularly true of shallow Lake Erie, but Lake Ontario is showing definite signs of middle age. Even Lake Michigan is beginning to age; the tremendous populations that surround it are beginning to have their effect upon it. Potentially Lake Michigan may be in the most hazardous position of all, for little water flows through it. It is drained by the Straits of Mackinac at

the northern end and by the Chicago Drainage Canal at the southern end, and the inflow comes only from the rivers along its shores.

The least obvious type of pollution is thermal pollution, the heating of a body of water by artificial means. The results also are the most debatable: does it actually do harm? Should it even be called pollution?

Heated water comes from industrial plants that draw water from the Lakes

for cooling and then pour it back into them. In theory, such a discharge will damage the natural balance of the lake that receives it by raising the temperature. Warmer water contains less oxygen, and if it is warm enough it will suffocate some forms of life. Species that are encouraged by warmer water are those that use less oxygen and that we generally consider less desirable, such as carp and catfish. And warmer water encourages the growth of seaweed and algae, which we certainly do not need.

That is the theory, and there is little question but that large doses of hot water will bring about exactly those conditions. But there is a very great question as to how extensive and how hot the water must be to cause trouble. Experiments by the prestigious Battelle Memorial Institute, a worldwide technical and scientific contract-research organization, indicate that the addition of warm water does not always do harm. On the Connecticut River, for example, a nuclear power plant that returns water

Another steel mill on the Cuyahoga pours its wastes into the river.

As warm water from a coal-fired electric generating station (behind the viewer) strikes the cold water of Lake Superior, vapor rises. Typical Lake Superior ore dock in the background.

heated some twenty degrees above the normal river temperature has not disturbed the annual spring runs of shad. The numbers of catfish, shiners, perch, and similar fish have increased at the place where the warm water enters the river, but not elsewhere along it. Daniel Merriman, director of the Connecticut River Study, functioning from 1965 through 1972, prefers the term *calefaction* to the more common *thermal pollution*. It simply means "warming" and does not have the built-in prejudgment that heating is always harmful.

What will be the overall effect of such a plant as the Bruce Nuclear Power Development on Lake Huron north of the Ontario town of Kincardine? What will its four 800,000-kilowatt units do toward heating the water? No one really knows. That statement echoes in the background as we do so many things to the Lakes. No one really knew what damage the mercury would cause. We found that out the hard way. How much better it would be if more studies such as the Connecticut River project could first be completed, so that we know what hot water probably will do, before we pour more and more of it into the Great Lakes.

In our daily environment, milk comes in paper cartons, meat is delivered in frozen portions, and sewage disappears at the touch of a lever. Most people never see the inside of a dairy farm, a slaughterhouse, or a sewage disposal plant. Our custom of pushing the less tidy aspects of our humanity into remote corners makes for a more pleasant existence, but it also makes for the dangerous illusion that we are nearer to angels than we are. We begin to think that somehow we are outside the biologic framework of life.

We ignore that framework at our peril, as nearly every example of pollution shows. The man who gags at the heavy chlorine in his drinking water is learning this lesson in a mild way; the one who dies of mercury poisoning from the fish he eats has no further need for learning. Our pollution problems stem from ignoring the natural processes or from overwhelming them. The dumping of mine tailings into Lake Superior or beer cans into Lake Ontario simply ignores the natural processes; the flow of sewage into the Lakes once made use of natural processes, but today with our current populations it can only overwhelm them.

Our problems can at least be moderated if we move in step with nature. A basic natural principle is the reuse of material. Nothing in nature is ever thrown away. In the Muskegon plan for sewage disposal we are starting to follow this principle. Manufacturers who are beginning to take pop bottles or old cars and rework them are experimenting gingerly with it. The immediate cost in both areas may well be greater than before, but in the larger view it will be cheaper than drowning in our own filth.

We should remember that in nature, bigger is seldom better. Our booming populations and our sprawling cities remind us of the mammoths and dinosaurs, monsters that did not survive. Until recently, large populations did not survive either. They were cut down by disease, famine, war, and disaster. By making large gains against the first two and some against the third and even fourth, we have kept alive great numbers of people who otherwise would have died. By neglecting to modify their breeding habits, our enlarged populations still have offspring at the rates once necessary to keep the species ahead of death. And those offspring survive and have their own large numbers of offspring; and thus we have the population explosion. If we cannot now bring ourselves and nature into balance, nature will surely do it for us. And nature is unforgiving to those who make mistakes, as many a man has found who went into the desert without enough water.

Barry Commoner, director of the Center for the Biology of Natural Systems at Washington University, Saint Louis, gives four basic laws of ecology:

(1) Everything is connected to everything else.
(2) Everything must go somewhere.
(3) Nature knows best.
(4) There is no such thing as a free lunch.

The first two laws are obvious statements of what we already know but often ignore. The third law is one that we are just beginning to understand.

Lagoon separated from Lake Erie by a sand bar. A high concentration of septic tanks in a nearby summer colony drain into the lagoon, with the results seen here and a smell that the picture does not register.

Dr. Commoner's researches show that since 1946, production in the United States has increased only at about the same rate as population, but that pollution has increased much more sharply. His further analysis shows, however, that within the overall activity of production there have been drastic changes during that time. The production of nonreturnable bottles increased 53,000 percent. That of synthetic fibers is up nearly 6,000 percent. Plastics and resins have increased nearly 2,000 percent and nitrogen fertilizers over 1,000 percent. Synthetic organic chemical products (such as detergents) are up 950 percent. There are comparable decreases in the production of returnable bottles, cotton and wool, soap, and other goods that have been displaced. The point, of course, is that we now have switched to manufacturing things that do not occur naturally, or that occur in nature only in small quantities. They are things that nature cannot break down. Once they have served their momentary purposes they go on forever, either inertly, like plastics and synthetic fibers, overwhelming us with our trash piles, or more actively, like fertilizers and detergents, throwing the ecological machinery drastically out of adjustment. In all of these areas man has thought that he could improve on nature, but instead he has been working at cross purposes with natural forces that are stronger than he is.

The fourth law sums up the impact of the other three, and it is the one that really hurts. Whatever we do has its cost, whether in dollars or in quality of environment.

In the past we have almost always spent the environment in order to save the dollars. Usually it was a bad bargain. Now we will have to spend more dollars to save the limited environment that remains. "We" of course means literally all of us, for large-scale costs in the final analysis are paid by taxpayers and consumers. Pollution control has already forced some paper companies to raise prices. In order to clean up the western end of Lake Erie, defiled mainly by Detroit, we may well have to pay more for Detroit's cars. Nearly everything on the shores of the Lakes (and on those of other lakes, and rivers, and oceans) is likely to cost more. To quote Joseph Wood Krutch again, "Ask an economist if we can afford to do what would be necessary to reverse the current trends, and he will certainly answer 'No.' Ask the ecologist if we can afford *not* to do so, and he also will answer 'No.' In a sense, both are right."

Yet here too, when we look not only at the gross cost of cleaning up pollution — which can appear staggering — but also at the cost per person, the sacrifice does not seem too great. In paper mills, the cost of effective waste treatment varies from two dollars to five dollars per ton of paper that they make. Newsprint, for example, is worth about $150 per ton. A newspaper may weigh about one pound; hence the reader would have to pay only a cent more each week to underwrite pollution control. Considering only that particular part of an auto provided by the steel industry, if 5 percent more for pollution control was added to the basic cost of steel, about $7.50 would be added to the cost of a one-ton car. Of course other products go into cars and they require further manufacturing, all of which adds costs; and of course the auto companies help pay taxes which build improved sewage systems. But fifteen dollars or even twenty-five dollars more per car seems a cheap price for clean water. Experts feel that an overall rise in costs of between 1 and 5 percent could well control pollution. We have become used to annual wage increases of 5 to 15 percent, which are promptly passed on to the consumer. By comparison, pollution control looks like a bargain.

In the future we must discover in advance what the effects of our activities will be upon the Lakes. Often we have not foreseen the results of a given action — witness the mercury mess. Worse could happen. Our ability to judge the

The Toledo sewage disposal plant recently installed this equipment to remove phosphate from sewage. Shown here under construction.

results of what we do may be helped in the future by a U.S. government effort to develop marine resources, called the National Sea Grant Program. Two of the bodies working with it in the Great Lakes area are the universities of Michigan and Wisconsin. In 1968, they started gathering data about the Lakes and

the biological, physical, and social forces in and around them.

Canada has gone a step further and has established on the Lakes the Canada Centre for Inland Waters, an organization whose duties range from charting inland waterways to public health matters. Its headquarters and extensive laboratories are at Burlington, on Lake Ontario — coincidentally or otherwise just across a small bay from the steel mills of Hamilton that give off wastes into both air and water. The Canada Centre has two ships, the *Limnos,* built as a floating laboratory, and the *Martin Karlsen,* a converted whaling ship; both are active on the Lakes. The *Karlsen,* for example, made a careful monitoring cruise of Lake Erie following a major storm in the summer of 1971 and charted the oxygen level at points throughout the lake, finding that the storm had so churned up the waters that the polluted, oxygen-depleted regions for a time lay mainly along the northern shore instead of the southern as usual. When newsmen asked the Cleveland office of the U.S. Environmental Agency about these findings, it replied that because of budgetary limitations it had not been able to do any sampling in Lake Erie that year.

Bodies such as the Canada Centre and the two universities hope that before long they can provide information for in-

The Canada Centre for Inland Waters operates size-able laboratories and two ships that constantly check water conditions. Here one of them, a former whaler, is tied up at the Burlington, Ontario, pier of the Centre. Across the bay the steel mills of Hamilton pour wastes into air and water.

telligent management of our natural resources. This management has been compared to a skillful game of chess: the player must know in advance just what each move that he makes will do to the entire playing board.

But even though we finally learn what are the wisest moves, will we be willing to take them? Political leaders who preach sacrifice are not those likeliest to be reelected. Our nation of individualists will not easily be persuaded to stop polluting their environment; hence some form of policing will no doubt be necessary. Yet many of the people who call most fervently for a better environment would be the first to rebel against a pollution police force that had authority to check *their* incinerators and septic tanks. It may well be that social organization to carry out wise actions will be harder to achieve than the technical ability to learn what actions are wise. It may even be that serious moves will not be accepted until there is a serious disaster.

Perhaps not, however. If the present interest in ecology is more than a fad, if responsible industries such as those in Muskegon are willing to take expensive control measures, and particularly if we, the public, are willing to bear our relatively small share of the costs and sacrifices, it may still be possible to clean up the Great Lakes.

Cliffs and breaking waves, Lake Superior. Vast scenes of natural beauty such as this provide one of the challenges for the intelligent management of our natural resources.

Wild ducks swimming.

Credits

Particular thanks are due Phrixos B. Papachristidis, who kindly invited me to spend three weeks aboard one of his vessels while it made a round trip through the Seaway and the Great Lakes, and to R. C. Truax, vice-president of the Papachristidis Company, who made the detailed and somewhat complicated arrangements.

Captain Gilles de Villers, First Officer Donald Langlois, and the other officers and crew members of the *Grande Hermine* were most gracious and did everything possible to provide information and make opportunities for me to gather material during the voyage.

I am most grateful to John H. Neil, Director of Laboratories for the Ontario Water Resources Commission, for reading parts of the book in manuscript and making a number of detailed and helpful suggestions, as well as for providing some of the specific data on fisheries and pollution; and to Eugene M. Simons, Fellow, Nuclear Systems Division, of Battelle Memorial Institute, Columbus, Ohio, for reading those parts of the book dealing with power and suggesting changes and clarifications.

Albert G. Ballert of the Great Lakes Commission gave kind permission to use the perspective map of the Seaway that he drew and offered encouragement in completing the book. Leonard J. Goodsell of that same body generously furnished extensive material on the Seaway as it is today and may be tomorrow, and on the water resources of the Great Lakes area. J. M. Scovic of Midland, Michigan, provided information about the Industrial Users Group. The public relations staffs of the Saint Lawrence Seaway Authority and the Saint Lawrence Seaway Development

Little pines.

Anchorage.

Corporation were unfailingly helpful. James O. Castagnera, Public Information Officer of the U.S. Ninth Coast Guard District, Cleveland, cheerfully answered questions about shipping and provided much information on winter navigation.

P. C. Walker of Shell Canada provided information about the Seaway and Lake shipping and most helpfully obtained additional information for my use. Captain Clarke of Port Cartier, Quebec, arranged for me to tour the facilities of his port, and Ernest Laycock was a highly informed guide.

Oliver T. Burnham of the Lake Carriers' Association and Lawrence A. Pomeroy, Jr., of the Great Lakes Historical Society gave freely of guidance, information, and helpful suggestions. Sir James Easton furnished a copy of his detailed study of freight movement in the Lakes region, plus additional information on power consumption. A. E. Wanket of the Detroit District, Corps of Engineers, provided material on extension of the navigational season.

Grateful thanks go to G. P. Keating of Canada Steamship Lines, Montreal, and R. A. Charman of the Hamilton office of that company, who provided an explanation of the package freight trade, the operations of the Hamilton package freight terminal, and a tour of that facility and of the package freighter *Fort William.*

T. A. Winkel, steamship superintendent of the Chesapeake and Ohio Railway, Ludington, Michigan, very helpfully provided information about railroad car ferries and suggested other sources of information about them.

Mrs. Elizabeth Gabis, Ross G. Fitchett, and L. Price of the Port of Toronto provided much useful information; and W. N. Mitchell, during a lengthy tour of Toronto harbor facilities, added greatly to my education on cargo handling. Robert E. Malcolmson of the Port of Hamilton kindly gave an extended tour of that harbor. Mark Sweeney and Kenneth Cherry provided a briefing and tour of the Toledo–Lucas County Port facilities; William Bueschen, of the Toledo coal-loading facility, was also interested and helpful. The public relations staff of the Chicago Port were helpful in giving information about their harbor. Miss Beverly J. Strike of the Port of Milwaukee provided much information and arranged for a tour of the harbor in the company of C. E. Swinford, Harbor Master, whose informative courtesy was of great help. J. L. Haskell, Deputy Port Director, kindly furnished additional information.

W. A. Webster and Fred Crew of the Collingwood Shipyard were most gracious in providing information, discussing ship design and construction, and showing me through the yard. Alan E. Law and Miss Penny Mitchell of Erie Marine arranged for me to see that shipyard, and Larry Harrison gave me an extensive tour and thorough explanation of its construction facilities and of the first thousand-foot freighter, the *Stewart J. Cort*. The American Shipbuilding Company kindly permitted me to go aboard the freighter *Roger Blough* in their Lorain yard and take pictures of her.

Ty Cross of Consumers Power Company (Michigan) and D. T. Wilkinson of Ontario Hydro provided much information about electric power in their respective areas. Howard A. Cummins of Buckeye Power discussed the problems of power companies and provided information about power during the course of a very pleasant evening.

Miss Janet Coe Sanborn of the Cleveland Public Library (who is also editor of the invaluable quarterly, *Inland Seas*) provided an extensive bibliography on Great Lakes pollution and ecology. A. R. Kirby of the Canada Centre for Inland Waters gave information on that organization and on polluted conditions in the Great Lakes.

Robert S. Bowman and L. J. Petarka, sanitary officers of Lucas and Ashtabula counties respectively (the counties at the northwestern and northeastern corners of Ohio, on the shores of Lake Erie), courteously gave advice and guidance on finding evidences of pollution in those counties. Robert O'Connell and Emil Hauser of the city of Toledo arranged for me to tour the Toledo sewage

Marsh scene with reflected clouds.

disposal plant — one of the best on the Great Lakes — under the able guidance of Robert Imo, who explained the processes of sewage disposal and the new equipment that was then being installed to cope with such problems as phosphate removal.

Numerous other people, on the shores of all of the Lakes, were helpful in answering questions and in providing opportunities for photographs.

To my wife Anne goes credit for the title of the book, as well as for being inspiration, critic, copyreader, guard against interruptions, companion on most of the trips required, and the main reason that the book was completed on time and in reasonable form.

Marquette Lighthouse, Lake Superior.

Photographic Note

Most of the color pictures in this book were taken with Leicas (an M-2, M-3, and M-4) and an assortment of lenses ranging from 35mm through 50 and 90mm to 135mm. The 35mm and 90mm were the two most often used. These cameras were supplemented with a Nikkormat FTN equipped as needed with a 300mm lens or a 20mm lens.

I often used a Rollei 35, a camera that is about the size of a pack of cigarettes, but that takes a full-frame 35mm picture. When going up or down the side of a ship on a forty-foot ladder it is pleasant to have a camera that can be put into a pocket and forgotten for the moment. On more normal occasions it also is convenient, when most of one's cameras are loaded with back-and-white film, to have in addition a compact camera loaded with color that can be brought into play when there suddenly appears a good color shot.

The color film used most frequently in all these cameras was Kodachrome-X. Next in frequency came Ektachrome-X, and then in special cases High-Speed Ektachrome rated at a speed of 400.

Black-and-white pictures were taken with cameras ranging from an Olympus Pen F half-frame camera, using both the normal 38mm lens and the excellent 50-90mm zoom lens, through the Leicas and the Nikkormat, to the now unfashionable but still versatile twin-lens Rolleiflex with f 2.8 taking lens. In a few cases the 300mm Nikkor lens was fitted with a 2x extender, giving the effect of a 600mm lens. Many of the black-and-whites were taken with the Nikkormat and a 43-86 zoom lens.

In the half-frame camera I used both Plus-X and Tri-X film. Tri-X was the black-and-white film used most often in the full-frame 35mm cameras. In the twin-lens Rollei I used Plus-X Pan Professional. The Tri-X was usually rated at an index of 400, but for some dim-light shots it was rated at 800. Plus-X in both sizes was rated at 125. Many of the sunny-day Tri-X shots were made through orange filters,

Goderich Lighthouse, Lake Huron.

and a few were made with a polarizing filter; some of the twin-lens reflex pictures were also made with a polarizing filter.

All of this may give the impression that I went about loaded down with a mountain of equipment. Sometimes that seemed to be true, but most of the pictures were taken over a two-year period and normally I used only one or two cameras at a time.

Most of the black-and-white developing and most of the printing of the initial black-and-white enlargements were done by Frank Bath of Watson's Studio, Midland, Ontario, whose help and advice greatly eased preparation of the book.

Pompous gull.

Bibliography

DOWN TO THE SEA

Aitken, Hugh G. J. *The Welland Canal Company.* Cambridge, Mass.: Harvard University Press, 1954.

Aug, Stephen M. "The Seaway After 10 Years — Tempered Optimism." In *The Sunday Star* (Washington, D.C.), June 29, 1969.

Ballert, Albert G., and Goodsell, Leonard J. "Decade of Progress: The Saint Lawrence Seaway 1959–1969." In *Limnos,* Summer 1969.

Benford, Harry, and Kilgore, Ullman. *Great Lakes Transport: Technological Forecast and Means of Achievement.* Ann Arbor: University of Michigan College of Engineering, 1969.

Blower, William, Jr. "That 50,000th Ton." In *Seaway Review,* Winter 1970/71.

Bonnycastle, Sir Richard. *Canada and the Canadians.* London, 1846.

Carr, D. Wm. & Associates, Ltd. *The Seaway in Canada's Transportation: An Economic Analysis.* 2 vols. Ottawa: The St. Lawrence Seaway Authority, 1970.

Doan, H. D. "Industry Moves in to Fight for a Sane Seaway Policy." In *Seaway Review,* Summer 1971.

Easton, Sir James. *Transportation of Freight in the Year 2000, with Particular Reference to the Great Lakes Area.* Detroit: The Detroit Edison Co., 1971.

Graves, Brig. Gen. Ernest. "Economics of Seaway Extension." In *Seaway Review,* Summer 1971.

Hazard, John L. *The Next Decade, 1969–1979, St. Lawrence Seaway.* Ann Arbor: Great Lakes Commission, n.d.

Hills, B. L. "A Light in the Darkness." In *Seaway Review,* Autumn 1970.

Howard, Craig. "Lakes Feeder Service Slated: Will Be Fully Containerized." In *New York Journal of Commerce,* July 26, 1971.

Hyatt, Jim. "Dire Straits: St. Lawrence Seaway, Completing 10th Year, Is Awash in Problems." *The Wall Street Journal,* December 12, 1969.

Lake Log Chips (Bowling Green State University). June 6, 1972, "Wartsila Shipbuilding Company."

Mabee, Carlton. *The Seaway Story.* New York: The Macmillan Company, 1961.

Port of Toronto News. March, 1972, "More 'Big Boxes' for the Great Lakes."

_____. April, 1972, "Year 2000 Projection a 'Copout.' "

_____. April, 1972, "The Seabag."

Breaking waves and birch tree.

The St. Lawrence Seaway Authority. *1969 Report, Tenth Anniversary.* Ottawa, 1970.

The St. Lawrence Seaway Development Corporation. *1969 Annual Report.* Washington, D.C., 1970.

Schaefer, Edward. "Seaway's Effect — Duluth Is Not Yet a Boom Town." In *Minneapolis Star,* June 27, 1969.

Seaway Review. Summer 1970, "The Slings and Arrows."

————————. Autumn 1970, "Europe Looks at Containerization."

U.S. Army Engineer District, Detroit, Corps of Engineers. *Survey Report on Great Lakes and Saint Lawrence Seaway — Navigation Season Extension.* Detroit, 1969.

U.S. Coast Guard. *Welcome Aboard U.S.C. G.C. Mackinaw.* Cleveland: Ninth Coast Guard District, n.d.

Volpe, John A. "Policy for the Seaway." In *Seaway Review,* Summer 1970.

Wilson, George E. "Breaking the Ice Barrier." In *Seaway Review,* Spring 1970.

————————. "Season Extension for America's Fourth Coast." In *Seaway Review,* Winter 1970/71.

————————. "The Seaway Development Corporation Looks at Season Extension." In *Seaway Review,* Summer 1971.

THE LAKERS

Barcus, Frank. *Freshwater Fury.* Detroit: Wayne State University Press, 1960.

Benford, Harry. "A Prognosis for Great Lakes Shipping." A lecture given in December 1970 at the Annual Meeting of the Great Lakes Historical Society.

Benford, Harry, and Kilgore, Ullman. *Great Lakes Transport: Technological Forecast and Means of Achievement.* Ann Arbor: University of Michigan College of Engineering, 1969.

Beukema, Christian. "The Demonstration: U.S. Steel Shipping, Winter 1970–71." In *Seaway Review,* Summer 1971.

Cargill News. August-September 1969, "Dakota Wheat and Superships."

Castagnera, James O. "Icebreaking Operations During the Winter of 1971-72 on the Great Lakes." In *Coast Guard News,* Ninth U.S. Coast Guard District, December 3, 1971.

Cleveland Plain Dealer. July 15, 1970. "Shipping News."

————————. May 6, 1972, "*Cort* Cargo Sets Record for Lakes."

Defoe, William, and Benford, Harry. "Michigan's Interest in Marine Transportation and in Extending the Operating Season" (paper). Ann Arbor: Department of Naval Architecture and Marine Engineering, University of Michigan, n.d.

Easton, Sir James. *Transportation of Freight in the Year 2000, with Particular Reference to the Great Lakes Area.* Detroit: The Detroit Edison Co., 1971.

Ellis, William D. *The Cuyahoga.* New York: Holt, Rinehart, and Winston, 1966.

Greenwood, John O. *Namesakes of the Lakes.* Cleveland: Freshwater Press, 1970.

————————. *Greenwood's Guide to Great Lakes Shipping, 1971.* Cleveland: Freshwater Press, 1971.

Hilton, George W. *The Great Lakes Car Ferries.* Berkeley: Howell-North Books, 1962.

Rocky island.

Krappinger, Odo. *Great Lakes Ore Carrier Economics and Preliminary Design.* Ann Arbor: Department of Naval Architecture and Marine Engineering, University of Michigan, 1966.

Lake Carriers' Association. *Annual Report,* editions 1968–70. Cleveland, 1969-71.

Landon, Fred. "Loss of the Western Reserve." In *Inland Seas,* Winter 1964.

Marine Historical Society of Detroit. *Ahoy and Farewell.* Detroit, 1970.

Runzel, Neil. "Downbound." In *Coast Guard News,* Ninth U.S. Coast Guard District, March 10, 1971. (Season extension.)

Seaway Review. Winter 1971/72, "Special Report: The 1972 Season Demonstration Program Gets Underway."

Toledo Blade. July 14, 15, 1970, "Eastcliffe Hall."

HARBORS AND SHIPYARDS

Baine, Richard P., and McMurray, A. Lynn. *Toronto: An Urban Study.* Toronto: Clarke Irwin, 1970.

Baker, Alden. "The Endless Problems of Designing Tomorrow's 50-Mile Metro Waterfront." In *The Globe and Mail* (Toronto), August 18, 1970.

——————. "Citizens' Groups Mobilize as Pollution Threatens Chicago's Waterfront." In *The Globe and Mail,* August 20, 1970.

Board of Harbor Commissioners, City of Milwaukee. *Directory of Great Lakes-Overseas Shipping Services.* Milwaukee, 1971.

——————. *Transit Time Study on 228 Voyages.* Milwaukee, 1971.

——————. *World Ports of Call Made Direct from the Port of Milwaukee.* Milwaukee, 1971.

——————. *Interesting Highlights about the Port of Milwaukee.* Milwaukee, n.d.

——————. *Port of Milwaukee.* Encino, Calif.: Windsor Publications, n.d.

Brockel, Harry C. "Great Lakes Ports Face Formidable Challenges." In *Seaway Review,* Spring 1970.

Brown, Sheldon S. "The Lime Island Bubbler System: A Season Extension Experiment," In *Seaway Review,* Spring 1972.

Burke, Thomas C. "Coming Soon, Year-Round Port Operation." In *Seaway Review,* Winter 1970/71.

Clery, Val. "Some Old Battleships Never Die." In *The Globe and Mail Magazine* (Toronto), August 7, 1971.

De Crane, Ray. "American Ship Buying Litton's Yard." In *Cleveland Press,* September 3, 1971.

Detroit Marine Historian. May 1971, "The Log."

Dickerson, Ray C. "Illinois International." In *Seaway Review,* Spring 1971.

Easton, Sir James. *Transportation of Freight in the Year 2000, with Particular Reference to the Great Lakes Area.* Detroit: The Detroit Edison Co., 1971.

Ellis, William D. *The Cuyahoga.* New York: Holt, Rinehart, and Winston, 1966.

Hamilton Harbour Commissioners. *Seaway Service Via Port of Hamilton.* Hamilton, Ont., 1969.

——————. *1969 Annual Report.* Hamilton, Ont., 1970.

Inland Seas. Spring 1971, "Changes in Name and Operation."

New York Times, International Edition. "Seaport of Chicago" (advertising supplement), September 19, 1966.

Ontario Hydro. *The Gifts of Nature.* Toronto, 1970.

——————(D. T. Wilkinson). Letter. Toronto, January 12, 1971.

——————. *Perspective.* Toronto, n.d.

Pomeroy, Lawrence A., Jr. "Great Lakes Calendar." In *Inland Seas,* Summer 1971.

Port of Chicago. *Annual Report — 1969, Seaport of Chicago.* Chicago, 1970.

——————. *Steamship Services.* Chicago, 1970.

Seaway Review. Winter 1970/71, "Lake Port Tonnage Survey."

——————. Spring 1971, "We Can Keep Our Harbors Open."

Sigurdson, Albert. "Shipping Notes." In *The Globe and Mail,* July 22, 1971.

Thunder Bay Chamber of Commerce. *Thunder Bay, Ontario, Canada.* Thunder Bay, 1970(?).

Toledo-Lucas County Port Authority. *Port of Toledo, U.S.A.* (Factual portifolio.) Toledo, n.d.

Toronto Harbour Commissioners. *A Bold Concept.* Toronto, 1968.

——————. *Annual Report for the Port of Toronto, 1969.* Toronto, 1970.

——————. *Annual Report for the Port of Toronto, 1970.* Toronto, 1971.

——————. "Full Containerization Comes to the Great Lakes." In *Port of Toronto News,* August, 1971.

——————. *Port of Toronto.* (Factual portfolio.) Toronto, n.d.

Upper Lake Superior Travel Council. *Thunder Bay, Ontario.* Thunder Bay, 1970(?).

Valpy, Michael. "For Years It's Been a Question of Smell." In *The Globe and Mail,* August 6, 1971.

POWER

Arnold, Dean E. "Thermal Pollution, Nuclear Power, and the Great Lakes." In *Limnos,* Spring 1970.

Consumers Power Company. *Annual Report 1969.* Jackson, Mich. 1970.

——————(Ty Cross). Letter. Jackson, September 29, 1971.

Copeland, Richard. "Selenium: the Unknown Pollutant." In *Limnos,* Winter 1970.

Detroit Edison Company. *Energy Consumption in the Urban Detroit Area During the Past Twenty-five Years.* Detroit, 1965(?).

Environment. July/August 1971, "Spectrum."

Merriman, Daniel. "The Calefaction of a River." In *Scientific American,* May 1970.

Michigan Energy Survey Committee. *Energy and the Michigan Economy: a Forecast.* Ann Arbor: Graduate School of Business Administration, University of Michigan, 1967.

Ontario Hydro. *The Gifts of Nature.* Toronto, 1970.

——————. *1969.* Toronto, 1970.

——————. *Hydroscope, Special Report.* Toronto, n.d.

——————. *Perspective.* Toronto, n.d.

———. *A Special Report on Nuclear Power*. Toronto, 1969.

Smithsonian. May, 1972, "Two Wrongs May Make a Right." (Selenium negating toxic effects of mercury.)

Stein, Jane. "A Hot Debate, Generated by Hot Water." In *Smithsonian*, June 1971.

Wilford, John Noble. "Power Shortage in U.S. . . . Part of a National Energy Crisis." In *New York Times* Service, July 20, 1971.

Winter, Ralph E. "Unready Kilowatts." In *The Wall Street Journal*, June 9, 1971.

FISHES AND FISHERIES

Applegate, Vernon C., and Van Meter, Henry D. *A Brief History of Commercial Fishing in Lake Erie*. Washington, D.C.: U.S. Fish and Wildlife Service, 1970. (Fishery Leaflet 630.)

Baldwin, Norman S., and Saalfeld, Robert W. *Commercial Fish Production in the Great Lakes, 1867–1960*. Ann Arbor: Great Lakes Fishery Commission, 1962. With Supplement, 1970.

Beeton, A. M. *Statement on Pollution and Eutrophication of the Great Lakes*. Milwaukee: Center for Great Lakes Studies, the University of Wisconsin — Milwaukee, 1970. (Special Report No. 11.)

Bligh, E. Graham. "Great Lakes Fish as Human Food." In *Limnos*, Spring 1971.

Department of Fisheries of Canada. *Lamprey Control and the Great Lakes*. Ottawa: The Queen's Printer, 1968.

Frick, Harold C. *Economic Aspects of the Great Lakes Fisheries of Ontario*. Ottawa: Fisheries Research Board of Canada, 1965.

Great Lakes Fishery Laboratory. *The Sea Lamprey and Its Control in the Great Lakes*. Ann Arbor: U.S. Fish and Wildlife Service, n.d.

International Joint Commission. *Pollution of Lake Erie, Lake Ontario, and the International Section of the St. Lawrence River*. Ottawa: The Queen's Printer, 1971.

Ludwig, James Pinson. "Great Lakes Gulls." In *Limnos*, Spring 1969.

McCaull, Julian. "Questions for an Old Friend." In *Environment*, July/August 1971.

McIvor, George H. *Report of Commission of Inquiry into Freshwater Fish Marketing*. Ottawa: The Queen's Printer, n.d.

Neil, John H. Letter on the subject of fisheries. Rexdale, Ont., October 22, 1971.

Ontario Department of Lands and Forests. *Commercial Fishing in Ontario*. Toronto, n.d.

Reinert, Robert E. "Insecticides and the Great Lakes." In *Limnos*, Fall 1969.

Schneider, R. Stephen. "Treating a Stream for Lamprey." In *Limnos*, Winter 1969.

Smith, Stanford H. "The Changing Ecology of Lake Erie." Talk given October 20, 1961, at the meeting of the Lake Erie Resource and Recreation Council.

———. "The Alewife." In *Limnos*, Summer 1968.

———. "Ectosystem Destruction in the Great Lakes and Possibilities for Reconstruction." Paper presented in April 1970 at the Fiftieth Anniversary Symposium, College of Fisheries, University of Washington.

———. "Trends in Fishery Management of the Great Lakes." Reprinted from *A Century of Fisheries in North America* (Nor-

Marblehead Lighthouse, Lake Erie. Built in 1823, this is the oldest light in continuous operations on the Lakes.

Shore and waves.

man G. Benson, ed.), American Fishery Society Special Publication No. 7, 1970.

⸻. "Species Interactions of the Alewife in the Great Lakes." In *Transactions of the American Fisheries Society,* Vol. 99, No. 4.

⸻. "Species Succession and Fishery Exploitation in the Great Lakes." In *Journal of the Fisheries Research Board of Canada,* Vol. 25.

Time. June 28, 1971, "Environment — The Case of the Missing Gulls."

BEACHES AND BOATS

Bluhm, Don. "The Brutal Chicago-Mackinac." In *Lakeland Boating,* February 1971.

Disturnell, J. *Sailing on the Great Lakes and Rivers of America.* Philadelphia, 1874.

Forster, John. *The Life of Charles Dickens.* Philadelphia, 1886.

Frohman, Charles E. *Sandusky's Yesterdays.* Columbus: The Ohio Historical Society, 1968.

⸻. *Put-in-Bay.* Columbus: The Ohio Historical Society, 1971.

The Globe and Mail (Toronto). July 23, 1971, "Ontario to Spend $18 Million in Developing Wasaga Recreational Resources."

Lakeland Boating. November-December 1969, "Fabulous Lake St. Clair."

Lime, David W. "Research for Determining Use Capacities of the Boundary Waters Canoe Area." In *Naturalist,* Spring 1971.

Littlejohn, Bruce M. "Quetico: Great Park or Timberman's Reserve?" In *Naturalist,* Spring 1971.

Newsweek. August 9, 1971, "Yachting for the Masses."

Pollard, James E., ed. *The Journal of Jay Cooke.* Columbus: The Ohio State University Press, 1935.

Richmond, John. "Cruising the Trent-Severn." In *Lakeland Boating,* June 1970.

Roe, Jim. "Cruising Lake Michigan." In *Yachting,* July 1971.

Rupp, Craig W. "Boundary Waters Canoe Area Management." In *Naturalist,* Spring 1971.

Thorndale, Theresa. *Sketches and Stories of the Erie Islands.* Sandusky, 1898.

West, Bruce. "Thorny Problem." In *The Globe and Mail,* August 18, 1971.

POLLUTION

Arnold, Dean E. "Thermal Pollution, Nuclear Power, and the Great Lakes." In *Limnos,* Spring 1970.

Bauer Engineering, Inc. *The Muskegon County Wastewater Management System,* Chicago, 1971.

Beamish, Richard J., and Harvey, Harold H. "Why Trout Are Disappearing in La Cloche Lakes." In *The Globe and Mail* (Toronto), July 26, 1971.

Beeton, A. M. *Statement on Pollution and Eutrophication of the Great Lakes.* Milwaukee: Center for Great Lakes Studies, the University of Wisconsin — Milwaukee, 1970.

Benarde, Melvin A. *Our Precarious Habitat.* New York: W. W. Norton & Co., Inc., 1970.

Canada Centre for Inland Waters. *Canada Centre for Inland Waters — 1970.* Burlington, Ont., 1971.

Claridge, Thomas. "Storm-Mixed Lake Erie

Waters Still Sick." In *The Globe and Mail,* August 25, 1971.

Cleveland Press. July 12, 1971, "Check the Beaches."

Commoner, Barry. *Science and Survival.* New York: Ballantine Books, 1970.

——————. "Soil and Freshwater: Damaged Global Fabric." In *Environment,* April 1970.

——————. "The Closing Circle." In *The New Yorker,* September 25 and October 2, 1971.

Copeland, Richard. "The Mercury Threat: Questions to Consider." In *Limnos,* Summer 1970.

Czaika, Sharon C. and Robertson, Andrew. "Unsung Heroes." In *Limnos,* Spring 1970.

Davies, J. Clarence, III. *The Politics of Pollution.* New York: Pegasus, 1970.

Dubos, Rene. "Standards of Living," In *Environment,* January/February 1972.

Environment. November 1970, "Spectrum."

Erlich, Paul R.; Holdren, John P.; and Commoner, Barry. "Dispute," In *Environment,* April 1972.

The Globe and Mail. August 24, 1970, "Mercury in Flesh of Lake St. Clair Ducks Is Twice Acceptable Level."

Goodsell, Leonard J. "Water Resources, Midwest." Paper read before the National Water Resources Engineering Meeting, Phoenix, Ariz., 1971. Ann Arbor: The Great Lakes Commission, 1971.

Gorham, Eville. "Air Pollution from Metal Smelters." In *Naturalist,* Autumn 1970.

International Joint Commission. *Pollution of Lake Erie, Lake Ontario, and the International Section of the St. Lawrence River.* Ottawa: The Queen's Printer, 1971.

Krutch, Joseph Wood. "If You Don't Mind My Saying So. . . ." In *The American Scholar,* Summer 1970.

Laycock, George. "Call It Lake Inferior." In *Audubon,* May 1970.

Limnos. Winter 1969, "An Exchange of Letters."

Merriman, Daniel. "The Calefaction of a River." In *Scientific American,* May 1970.

Neil, John H. Letter on the subject of pollution. Rexdale, Ont., October 20, 1971.

Ontario Hydro. *A Special Report on Nuclear Power.* Toronto, 1970.

Posten, H. W. "Defueling the Nordmeer." In *Limnos,* Winter 1969.

Reinert, Robert E. "Insecticides and the Great Lakes." In *Limnos,* Fall 1969.

Robertson, Andrew. "What Is Happening to Our Great Lakes?" In *Limnos,* Spring 1969.

Saddington, R. R. "How One Company Is Trying to Combat the Problems of Pollution." In *The Globe and Mail,* July 26, 1971.

Seagran, Harry L. "Mercury in Great Lakes Fish." In *Limnos,* Summer 1970.

Sewerage Commission of the City of Milwaukee. *Milwaukee Waste Water Treatment Facilities.* Milwaukee, n.d.

Sheaffer, John R. "Reviving the Great Lakes." In *Saturday Review,* November 7, 1970.

Stein, Jane. "A Hot Debate, Generated by Hot Water." In *Smithsonian,* June 1971.

Time. September 28, 1970, "The Mercury Mess."

U.S. Corps of Engineers, Department of the Army. *Alternatives for Managing Wastewater for the Cleveland-Akron Metropolitan and Three River Watershed Areas, Summary Report.* July 1971.

——————. *Alternatives for Managing Wastewater for Southeastern Michigan, Summary Report.* July 1971.

——————. *Interim Report of the Secretary of the Army on the Pilot Wastewater Management Program.* 1971.

Winchester, John W. "Pollution Pathways in the Great Lakes." In *Limnos,* Spring 1969.

Young, Gordon, and Blair, James P. "Our Ecological Crisis." In *National Geographic Magazine,* December 1970.

Canada Geese.

Index
Italicized numbers refer to pictures or picture captions

Jacket design by Nicholas Goff and typography and book design by Dan Van't Kerkhoff, Baker Book House Company, Grand Rapids, Michigan.

Type for text matter, 11 point Times Roman, set by Dickinson Brothers, Inc., Grand Rapids. Caption type, 9 point Helvetica Italic, set by Typographics, Inc., Grand Rapids.

Color separations, platemaking, and printing by Wynalda Litho, Rockford, Michigan. Text paper, S. D. Warren Casco Saxony, embossed finish, 100 lb.

Binding and stamping by John H. Dekker and Sons, Grand Rapids. Cloth, Bayside Chambray, by Columbia Mills.